A YEAR FULL OF

GRATITUDE

How to Turn Your Inner Critic Into Your Biggest Cheerleader

Clare Josa

First published by Beyond Alchemy Publishing in 2013, titled "Gratitude: A Daily Journal"

3rd Edition ISBN 978-1-908854-76-6

Cover Artwork: Dean Rush

Cover Design: Ces Rosanna Price www.inspiredtoinspire.co.uk

The advice in this book is intended for educational purposes only and it is not intended to substitute for professional medical advice. In the event that you use any of this information for yourself, the publisher and author accept no responsibility for your actions. Always consult your medical professional, if you are unsure about whether any of the suggested techniques are suitable for you.

Dedication

I dedicate this book to my boys.

May you laugh more than you cry and may your days be filled with sunshine.

And may this gratitude journal be a magic wand for you, in whichever way you want it to be.

Contents

Grab Your Readers' Club Bonuses NOW

Don't put it off – dive in right now to make the most of A Year Full Of Gratitude!

Here's where to grab your bonuses NOW!

www.ClareJosa.com/gratitudeclub

Here's Some Of What You'll Find In The Readers' Club:

Want more than a book? You've got it!

Learning happens best when you get to *experience* how something works, rather than just skim-reading it. That's why you've got the readers' club. In it, you'll find bonus videos, articles and MP3s to take you through key techniques. It's as close as I can make it to sitting on your sofa with you and guiding you, step by step, through your year full of gratitude.

Love one of the quotes or affirmations? Share it!

Each affirmation and quote comes with a beautiful graphic you can share on social media, to inspire your friends. Or you could print them out and stick them around your home to inspire your day.

Want some moral support? It's yours!

Your readers' club forum is there for you to share the journey with like-minded souls, to celebrate your successes and to get answers to your questions. It's your virtual accountability buddy, keeping you motivated and on-track.

Want a free upgrade to an interactive online course?

A Year Full Of Gratitude comes with its very own podcast, email and video course.

Join the readers' club today and you'll get a short email each week, sharing quick links to the resources in the readers' club for that week's topic, letting you know about the relevant companion podcast episode (which turns this book into a year-long online training course), and sharing tips, insights and resources that wouldn't fit in the book.

Here's where to grab your bonuses NOW!

www.ClareJosa.com/gratitudeclub

Getting The Most From Your Gratitude Journal

You will see these symbols at various points in your journal. They are there to let you know that it's a chance to go a bit deeper, if you want to. Here's what they mean:

Bonus Audios
Whenever you see this symbol, it means that there's an audio for that technique, over in the readers' club. I'll guide you through that technique, as though we were on a workshop together.

Podcast Episode
This book is a stand-alone self-study course. But if you want more background info for each week and extra ninja tips that wouldn't fit in here, then your ten-minute weekly podcast is essential – and hopefully inspirational - listening. **You will find the links to each episode in the readers' club.**

Bonus Articles & Videos
This means there's a bonus article, video or other resource, to help you take things to the next level or to give a deeper explanation of the topic. These are easy to find each week in your readers' club.

You Are Not Alone!
Share the journey! Get answers to your questions, be inspired by others and celebrate your successes with fellow readers, over in the readers' club forum.

Take A 'Snapshot'
This is a reminder to take another 'snapshot' (see page 12), so you can feel the progress you're making, spotting how gratitude is getting easier for you how your life is changing.

Join now: **www.ClareJosa.com/GratitudeClub**

More Than 'Just' A Gratitude Journal

This journal brings you so much more than 'just' space to write down things that you feel grateful for.

It is a year-long programme to retrain your brain to think more positively, to help you reclaim the power from your inner critic, and to shift that inner voice – one thought at a time – to become your biggest cheerleader.

My big dream for you, in writing this book and creating the accompanying readers' club and podcast, is to give you the tools to retrain your brain to think happier thoughts and to tame your inner critic, so you can walk around with a smile on your face, for no particular reason, and inspire those around you to do the same!

If at any stage the feelings of 'scary' or 'difficult' pop up for you, don't worry – it means you're about to stretch a comfort zone a little bit (or maybe even a lot). Make sure you pop into the readers' club forum for moral support. Similarly, whenever you have a 'lightbulb moment' or a breakthrough, it can be hard to explain it to those around us. That's where the readers' club forum comes into its own. By sharing your successes, you inspire others to create life-long shifts, too.

Every two weeks, you'll get a gratitude technique or conecept to play with. These are designed to build on each other, week by week, to help you go more deeply into experiencing gratitude, gently releasing any blocks and resistance and to inspire you along the journey.

If you don't do the project one week or if it doesn't resonate for you, that's ok. Just pick up with the next one. This is *your* journey. But do be aware that the techniques we avoid often hold the greatest gifts for us.

The affirmations are intended to help you to set your intention for the day. Each one covers two weeks. If you'd like to use some of your own, instead, that's fine. This is *your* journal.

And make sure you take a few minutes to listen to each week's podcast. These cover the background to key techniques plus ninja tips for when you're in the flow with a technique and want to take it to the next level, especially if you're dealing with negative self-talk and want to turn your inner critic into your biggest cheerleader.

If you write in your journal, most days, do each technique a few times, and listen to a good portion of the podcast episodes, then I promise you that in a year's time you will be a completely different person – and you will have transformed your experience of life.

Changing your life doesn't have to be difficult – so you might as well do it with a smile on your face and gratitude in your heart!

What On Earth Is 'Gratitude'?

Gratitude is so much more than a 'thank you' – though that is a great place to start. The dictionary defines 'gratitude' as:

The quality of being thankful; readiness to show appreciation for and to return kindness.

But that's not the kind of gratitude we're going for with this gratitude journal. The dictionary definition is about conditional gratitude – "Give me something and I'll say thank you." We are going to be experiencing full-blown, heart-opening, life-changing gratitude.

To balance the dictionary definition, I'd like to offer you a perspective of gratitude that might help you get a sense of what we'll be playing with this year:

Gratitude is a way of experiencing life from the perspective of love, rather than fear.

Starting from wherever you are currently 'at', **A Year Full Of Gratitude** will guide you along the way, starting with simple exercises to help you create a gentle gratitude habit, slowly retraining your brain to spot more of what is going well in life, rather than being stuck on the complaining train. The way the exercises build on each other means there's very little resistance – you'll get better results, faster and with less effort if you go through them in order. Over time, you'll move on to powerful techniques that can create beautiful, exciting and nourishing shifts in your experience of life, one thought at a time.

How Can Gratitude Help You?

When we view life through the filter of gratitude and love, rather than fear and worry, it impacts the world that we see. That's basic neuroscience, not woo-woo. We notice more things to feel grateful for. The tone of our thoughts shifts. Our actions change. Our relationships improve. Our cells rebalance and heal, improving our health. We start to see miracles taking place in the world around us.

I don't want to dictate to you how gratitude will help you this year. Instead, I invite you to tune your radar into noticing the shifts that gratitude creates for you – there's a 'snapshot' process on page 12 to help with this, as well as regular review points, throughout this journal. I will make you a promise though:

After working through this journal, over the coming year, consciously giving thanks each day for the abundance in your life, you will be a different – and even happier – person than you are today. Those around you will be asking you what your secret is!

Dealing With The #1 Life-Change Excuse, Once And For All

What's the number one excuse I hear people (and myself) using to avoid making changes in our lives?

"But I Don't Have Time!"

When you're stuck in the middle of 'doing' your old thoughts, feelings and habits, it can feel difficult to take the time out to stand back and become aware of which bits you want to change. Yet that time will repay you every single day, for the rest of your life.

We become so convinced by our lack-of-time excuses that there is no room left for us to change.

Would we rather spend the next fifty years going through the pain and hurt and everything else we currently feel - and all the 'dis-ease' that it brings with it – than dedicate a few minutes a day to making the shifts we want?

Is it really true that our lives are too full to find the time? Surely much of our time is used up by the very patterns we want to shift?

How To Magically Create The Time For Your Gratitude Practice

Whether you believe you have enough time or you believe you don't, you're right.

We believe our stories and excuses, telling them to ourselves so often that they become a pseudo-truth that we no longer question. But is it really true?

It's funny how, for example, if we fall in love, we suddenly find plenty of evenings and weekends to spend with that wonderful new person. We watch less TV; we read fewer magazines; we spend less time on the internet; we spend less time on chores; we use our time more intentionally; we work more efficiently; and we drop anything that's not essential.

Is it really too much for your mind, body and soul to ask for a few minutes of your time each day for something that can dramatically impact your life?

There are many 'important jobs' and distractions during the day that steal our time; things that crop up unexpectedly, to which we give our immediate attention. Everything else falls off the table, including the time we had set aside for working 'on ourselves'. Yet if we were to tell those distractions, "I'll come back to you later," it's amazing how they either go away or take up less time.

The classic example is a phone call. You're in the middle of something important, but you answer the phone anyway. The conversation takes ten minutes. Then you go back to what you were doing. You found ten minutes for the interruption. So why do we find it so hard to find even a few minutes to change our lives…? The week 0 podcast episode includes an exercise that can really help with this.

Little And Often

You will make better progress with your gratitude practices if you do them 'little and often', rather than blitzing them, once in a blue moon. That's the beauty of this journal – you are setting your intention to focus on gratitude every day, rather than twice a month. I encourage you to remind yourself, each day, to experiment with one (or more!) of these exercises, to allow them to create shifts in your experience of life.

Inspiration can give us the idea. Motivation can get us started.
But it's routine and habit that create the change.

My Top Tips For Finding More Time

1. Set a time for your gratitude journal and techniques, each day, and stick to it. Treat it like an appointment.

2. Be realistic. By all means set yourself a challenging goal on how many minutes a day you want to spend on this, but be realistic about your other commitments.

3. If something needs to drop off the table, to create the time you need, take action to make it happen.

4. If you need moral support, ask for it! Your family, friends and colleagues might surprise you.

5. Write you answer below: **How are you going to make sure you have time for your gratitude journal, every day?**

 If finding a few minutes a day to practise gratitude and write in this journal is an issue for you, there are extra resources and discussions waiting to help you, over in the readers' club forum in the section '**Before We Start**': www.clarejosa.com/gratitudeclub

Why write your gratitude down, rather than just doing it in your head?

Writing your gratitude down makes it feel more real. It becomes a more powerful signal to your unconscious mind that you want it to look for more things for which to feel grateful.

And it's easier to look back and review things you have written down! If you're having a tough day, your mind might struggle to remember happy stories. But if they're waiting for you in your gratitude journal, it can take you back to feeling more positive, nearly instantly.

Over the coming year, I'll be teaching you all kinds of wonderful ways to weave gratitude into your daily life. You can do it. Or you can choose not do it. That's up to you.

The main thing is that you 'get' that this journal won't work by 'osmosis'; by just sitting next to your bed: if you want to see results, you've got to use this stuff! That's why I have broken it down into bite-sized chunks – so that it's easy for you to change our life in less time than it takes a kettle to boil.

Just imagine the shifts you're going to make in your life in the coming
year!

This gratitude journal will transform your experience of life. To experience those shifts, here's what you need to do:

- **Write 3-5 things you feel grateful for in the journal, each day**
  It doesn't have to be an essay (there's not space for that!) Make brief notes or sketches (it doesn't have to be words, if that's not your thing) to capture what you're feeling grateful for. The foundation exercise – Gratitude Minutes on page 13 – will make this easy.

- **Use the affirmations.**
  Every couple of weeks you'll get a new affirmation – you'll see them at the top of each journal entry page. To allow these to create shifts for you, all you need to do is to say them, regularly, throughout your day.

  There are also inspiring (and sometimes provoking!) gratitude quotes, scattered throughout your journal. Many of these have beautiful images to go with them, in the Readers' Club. You can download large full-colour versions to print out and display in your home, if you wish, or share them with friends on social media.

- **Do the exercises!**
  Every two weeks you get another gratitude exercise. These are designed to help you really shift your experience of gratitude and to gently make lasting changes in your life. You could set a reminder on your phone at regular points during your day, so you get to play with these.

Now that's sorted… shall we begin?

How To Spot The Progress You're Making

It's easy to miss the changes we make in our lives. We're too busy 'doing the living' to notice them.

This journal comes with built-in 'spot your progress' techniques. By writing each day, you'll have journal entries to review. And every few weeks I encourage you to do a simple, yet effective, exercise that helps you to really notice the shifts you have been making. You will get to time to reflect and compare how you used to handle life 'in the olden days' with how you're handling it now.

It's important to allow yourself to spot those shifts – and to take a few moments to congratulate yourself on those changes. It's one of the keys to staying motivated.

Snapshot: Where Are You Now?

One of the easiest ways to notice the progress you're making is to learn to take a 'snapshot' – to notice 'where you're at' at the moment. If you do this every few weeks, you'll really see the shifts. There will be prompts in your journal, to remind you to do this.

Here are some simple questions that can help you to figure that out.

You might find it helps to write the answers down.

1. Which emotions do you feel most often, during a typical day?

2. How would you describe your stress levels?

3. What kinds of thoughts does your mind typically think?

4. How would you describe your energy levels and your physical health?

5. Why are you choosing to practise gratitude?

6. If you could make one change in your life, what would it be?

7. How will you know when you have made that change?

8. If you could give one piece of advice to yourself, right here, right now, what would it be?

 We will be coming back to this snapshot technique at regular points over the coming year. Whenever you see the 'pencil' symbol, it's a gentle reminder to come back and take another 'snapshot'. There will also be a discussion thread waiting for you in the readers' forum, to share what you noticed.

A YEAR FULL OF GRATITUDE

LET'S GET STARTED!

Foundation Exercise: Gratitude Minutes

Imagine being able to switch from grump to great – from stressed to smiling – in under sixty seconds! That is wah you'll be doing with your Gratitude Minutes practice. This is a foundation exercise for this journal, because you can do it every day, even when your main gratitude practice might be something else. It helps you to switch from grumpy to grateful – or wherever you didn't want to be, to gratitude – in a minute or two.

Over the coming months, we'll be building on this foundation exercise with gratitude techniques to take you through a life-changing journey, experiencing the how gratitude can retrain your inner critic. But for the first few weeks, these six steps are all I'm asking you to do.

Gratitude Minutes

1. **Take a deep breath and breathe out with a sighing 'ahhh' sound.**
   This helps you to let go of tension. Repeat 3 times, if you need to, to help you relax.

2. **Smile a gentle smile – a 'half-smile'.**
   'Half-smiling' helps you to let go of any stresses, to rebalance your body's sympathetic nervous system ('fight or flight' / adrenalin) with your parasympathetic nervous system (relaxation) and it gently starts the releasing of endorphins – your body's natural 'feel good' hormones.

3. **Think of 3-5 things you feel grateful for.**
   It doesn't have to be 'big' or 'serious' – whatever comes to mind. Think of one at a time, pausing on each one for at least 10 seconds, allowing yourself to fully experience a sense of gratitude – an inner 'thank you' – for whatever it is. Then move on to the next one and the next one.

4. **Thank yourself.**
   Thank yourself for taking the time to practice gratitude today.

5. **Release the practice.**
   Let go of the practice. There's no need to analyse, critique, judge or tell yourself stories. It will most likely feel different each day. And that's ok. What matters is consistency – doing it as many days of the year as you can remember (hopefully this gratitude journal and the readers' club will help!).

6. **Write your answers down each day in the journal spaces.**
   Writing them down makes them feel even more real and creates a wonderfully uplifting resource if ever you're feeling down.

Affirmation:

I love the difference a minute can make.

Week 1: Day 1 ~ *Today I am grateful for…*   *Date:*

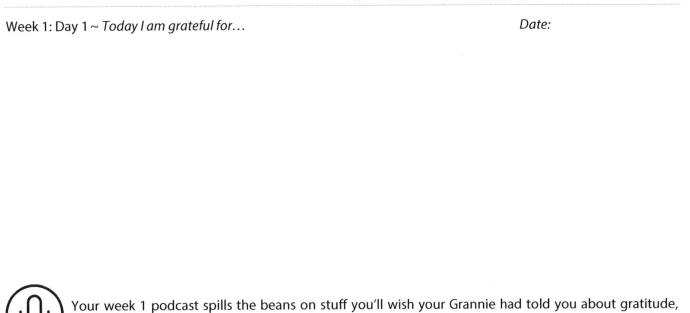

Your week 1 podcast spills the beans on stuff you'll wish your Grannie had told you about gratitude, plus the neuroscience behind why your Gratitude Minutes work so well.

Week 1: Day 2~ *Today I am grateful for…*   *Date:*

Affirmation: "I love the difference a minute can make."

Week 1: Day 3 ~ *Today I am grateful for…*   *Date:*

Week 1: Day 4~ *Today I am grateful for…*   *Date:*

Gratitude is more than a few nice words. It's a way of living. It opens your eyes to the wonder of life and opens your heart to love.

Week 1: Day 5 ~ *Today I am grateful for…*   *Date:*

Week 1: Day 6~ *Today I am grateful for…*   *Date:*

Week 1: Day 7 ~ *Today I am grateful for…*   *Date:*

Week 2: Day 1 ~ *Today I am grateful for...*   *Date:*

Your week two podcast covers how to use this week's Gratitude Minute technique to press near-instant 'pause' on your inner critic's mind-chatter.

Week 2: Day 2 ~ *Today I am grateful for...*   *Date:*

Week 2: Day 3 ~ *Today I am grateful for…*   *Date:*

Week 2: Day 4 ~ *Today I am grateful for…*   *Date:*

The Universe can't resist a grateful heart. The more you feel grateful for, the more you will find to feel grateful for.

Week 2: Day 5 ~ *Today I am grateful for…*   *Date:*

Week 2: Day 6 ~ *Today I am grateful for…*   *Date:*

Affirmation: "I love the difference a minute can make."

Week 2: Day 7 ~ *Today I am grateful for…*   *Date:*

Notes: What have you noticed so far? Any insights? Any questions? Let us know! There's a special week 2 discussion thread over in the readers' club: www.ClareJosa.com/GratitudeClub

Change Your Life With A Gratitude Jar

Here's one of my favourite Gratitude Projects, which you could start today and then let it work its magic all year:

A Gratitude Jar

1. Grab a jar – you can decorate it, if you like. Make it a big one!
2. Every few days, aim to write a short note to put in the jar with a few words on it about something you feel grateful for. It doesn't have to be anything big – whatever comes to mind.
3. Whenever you're having a bad day, dive into the jar and remind yourself how many things you have been feeling good about, over the year.
4. When the end of the year comes around, put some time aside to read through the messages in your jar and to experience what a wonderful year it has been.
5. Then start another jar, next year. You could put the old one in a special place, to keep for future generations of 'you'!

How about decorating your gratitude jar and posting a photo of it in the readers' club forum? Kids love this exercise, too!

Affirmation:

I enjoy finding things to feel grateful for.

Week 3: Day 1 ~ *Today I am grateful for…*   *Date:*

 Your week 3 podcast talks about how to handle 'gratitude stage fright' if your mind goes blank when you're doing your gratitude practice – it's surprisingly common!

Affirmation: "I enjoy finding things to feel grateful for."

Week 3: Day 2 ~ *Today I am grateful for…*   *Date:*

Week 3: Day 3 ~ *Today I am grateful for…*   *Date:*

Got gratitude stage fright? 3 quick starters:: (1) You can breathe, which (2) means you're alive so (3) you can Change your world.. What could you feel grateful for today?

Week 3: Day 4 ~ *Today I am grateful for…*   *Date:*

Week 3: Day 5 ~ *Today I am grateful for…*   *Date:*

Affirmation: "I enjoy finding things to feel grateful for."

Week 3: Day 6 ~ *Today I am grateful for...*   *Date:*

Week 3: Day 7 ~ *Today I am grateful for...*   *Date:*

Week 4: Day 1 ~ *Today I am grateful for…*   *Date:*

 Your week 4 podcast talks about 'gratitude wobbles' – if a technique brings up emotions for you that you had perhaps been avoiding. And it tells you how to release those hidden blocks and feel great again.

Week 4: Day 2 ~ *Today I am grateful for…*   *Date:*

You have the gift of 1,440 minutes today. Have you used one of them to say "thank you" yet?

Affirmation: "I enjoy finding things to feel grateful for."

Week 4: Day 3 ~ *Today I am grateful for…*   *Date:*

Week 4: Day 4 ~ *Today I am grateful for…*   *Date:*

Week 4: Day 5 ~ *Today I am grateful for…*   *Date:*

Week 4: Day 6 ~ *Today I am grateful for…*   *Date:*

Don't wait to say thank you for the big stuff. Start with the
smallest seed and watch the miracles grow.

Week 4: Day 7 ~ *Today I am grateful for…*   *Date:*

Pause for a moment to take a snapshot (see page 12). You can use this space to make any notes. And perhaps you'd like to share how you're getting on so far over at the readers' club forum? You can join the readers' club here: www.ClareJosa.com/GratitudeClub/

Bedtime Gratitude Spiral

For our next project, we're moving on to a variation of last week's Gratitude Minutes, but with a tweak that makes it a real treat. I call it a Bedtime Gratitude Spiral. Here's a quick tour of why it's so potent.

Sometimes it can feel hard to fall asleep. If we're feeling stressed or our mind is running over the events of the day, sleep can feel like a distant promise – and gratitude might well be the last thing on your mind. If you find that 'life' is keeping on going round and round in your head, the Bedtime Gratitude Spiral can help you to put those worries aside and move your thoughts to a happier space.

The last thing you think about at night – and the last emotion you're feeling – can have a major impact on the quality of your sleep.

It's as though those final pre-sleep thoughts give your mind an unconscious message about where to tune its radio station; about what to focus on for the next few hours. It takes this as an instruction to send you dreams that match the emotions you were feeling as you fell asleep. We often wake up still feeling those emotions.

Consciously creating a happy, grateful mood as you fall asleep can make a big difference.

It's easier than you might think. In fact, you've been training yourself to do it over the past few weeks.

It's not about pretending that everything is 'ok', even if you're convinced that it's not. It's not about 'rejecting' any worries or negative thoughts you have been having. It **is** about allowing happier thoughts to creep in and have centre stage for a few minutes. And one of the simplest and most effective ways to achieve this is to think of things that we feel grateful for.

1. **Before you fall asleep, choose three things you feel grateful for, to use for this exercise.**
   It might be something that happened during the day; it might be something from your gratitude jar. It doesn't matter what you choose, as long as it helps you to connect with the feeling of gratitude in your heart, even if it's only a glimmer.

2. **Allow yourself to gently rest in the feeling of gratitude for the first thing.**
   - Really experience the grateful emotion. Feel the gratitude expanding and growing. Don't force it; just let it naturally work its magic.
   - Really dive into the experience you are feeling grateful for. See what you would be seeing, if it were happening right now; hear what you would hear; feel the physical sensations that you would feel.
   - Allow the intensity of your gratitude to increase, perhaps imagining that you have a dial you can use to turn up the feeling, until it is spreading, like a warm golden glow, throughout your body. [... *continues*]

3. **If the feeling of gratitude starts to wane, move on to the second thing and repeat step 2.**
   Then, just as you notice it start to wane, move onto your third thing.

4. **You can keep going, if you want to, until you fall asleep.**

5. **Notice how your mood is shifted.**
   Perhaps say a heart-felt 'thank you' to yourself, for choosing to do the Bedtime Gratitude Spiral.

Just imagine how the quality of your sleep could improve, if you do this last thing at night?!

It can help to anchor this process into part of your bedtime routine, to help you remember to do it. For example, you could tie it in with turning off your light. If you read before you sleep, you could anchor it in with putting the book down. Or you could choose to do it when your head touches the pillow.

You only need to do this for a few days and already you'll be creating a life-long positive habit.

Affirmation:
I enjoy my gratitude minutes. They bring a smile to my face.

Week 5: Day 1 ~ *Today I am grateful for…*   *Date:*

 Your week 5 podcast talks about the two primary emotions that drive our thoughts, actions and even our results - plus the role that your daily gratitude practice plays in this.

Week 5: Day 2 ~ *Today I am grateful for…*   *Date:*

Week 5: Day 3 ~ *Today I am grateful for…*   *Date:*

Week 5: Day 4 ~ *Today I am grateful for…*   *Date:*

Week 5: Day 5 ~ *Today I am grateful for…*   *Date:*

Week 5: Day 6 ~ *Today I am grateful for...*   *Date:*

Week 5: Day 7 ~ *Today I am grateful for...*   *Date:*

Learning to live in gratitude is about gently, but firmly, retraining your mind to think thoughts that come from a place of love, rather than fear and worry.

Week 6: Day 1 ~ *Today I am grateful for…*   *Date:*

 Your week 6 podcast talks about how we can choose which thoughts to feed – which stories to tell – so that we are improving the *quality* of our thoughts – plus how this affects our performance.

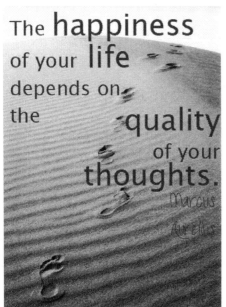

The **happiness** of your **life** depends on the **quality** of your **thoughts.** *Marcus Aurelius*

What have you noticed so far? Any shifts? Any insights? Care to share them at the readers' club forum? Here's some space for your notes:

Week 6: Day 2 ~ *Today I am grateful for…*   *Date:*

Week 6: Day 3 ~ *Today I am grateful for…*   *Date:*

Week 6: Day 4 ~ *Today I am grateful for…*   *Date:*

Week 6: Day 5 ~ *Today I am grateful for…*   *Date:*

Week 6: Day6 ~ *Today I am grateful for…*   *Date:*

Week 6: Day 7 ~ *Today I am grateful for…*   *Date:*

 I'm curious: what do you find it easy to feel grateful for? And what is it more difficult to feel grateful for? We're talking about this over in the readers' club: www.ClareJosa.com/GratitudeClub

The Secret To Keeping Yourself Motivated

Today you're getting one of my personal secrets for staying motivated, when I want to create a new habit. And I won't keep you in suspense:

The secret to keeping yourself motivated is knowing your "Big Why"

When you know why you want to do something, it's so much easier to find the time and energy to do it; to make those changes. Here's a simple exercise that can help you figure out your "Big Why" and how to make the most of it, to help keep you motivated over the coming year – and beyond.

Allow yourself a few minutes to think and write down your answers below these questions:

1.   Why have you keeping a gratitude journal?

2.   What do you hope that practising gratitude each day is going to do for you?

3.   How are you going to notice that it is working for you? Which behaviours, which signs, which emotions are you going to be tracking to feel the progress you are making?

4.   What kinds of barriers can you foresee that might get in the way of you finding a few minutes a day for your practice?

5.   Before you go any further with this project, what are you going to do about those barriers?

6.   Do you need to clear anything out of your schedule? Or ask for help? Or delegate something to create that time, a few minutes a day?

7.   If you *don't* make the most of this gratitude journey, what might happen?

8.   And let the answer to this next question bubble up gently for you – don't rationalise it... Complete the following sentence:

I choose to spend time focusing on gratitude each day, because...

And when you are ready, write that whole sentence up somewhere. Pin it up around your home or around your office. If you notice distractions getting in the way of your practice, you can remind yourself: "I choose to spend time focusing on gratitude each day, because......"

You might be surprised how often that helps you to prioritise your gratitude time over the distractions. How about sharing, over at the readers' club forum?

For the next two weeks, keep going with your gratitude minutes and bedtime gratitude spiral.

Affirmation:
I can feel how important gratitude is becoming in my everyday life.

Week 7: Day 1 ~ *Today I am grateful for…*   *Date:*

Your week 7 podcast is about the dangers of white-washing – sometimes called the 'spiritual bypass'. Your gratitude journey isn't about pretending everything's ok or denying life's brown stuff. Find out how to handle this – with gratitude - in the next ten minutes.

Week 7: Day 2 ~ *Today I am grateful for…*   *Date:*

Week 7: Day 3 ~ *Today I am grateful for…*   *Date:*

Week 7: Day 4 ~ *Today I am grateful for…*   *Date:*

Gratitude is a skill, just like any other we choose to develop. And
it takes practice. Use your journal to inspire your journey.

Week 7: Day 5 ~ *Today I am grateful for…*   *Date:*

Week 7: Day 6 ~ *Today I am grateful for…*   *Date:*

Week 7: Day 7 ~ *Today I am grateful for…*   *Date:*

Pause for a moment to take a snapshot (see page 12). You can use this space to make any notes. And perhaps you'd like to share how you're getting on so far over in the readers' club forum?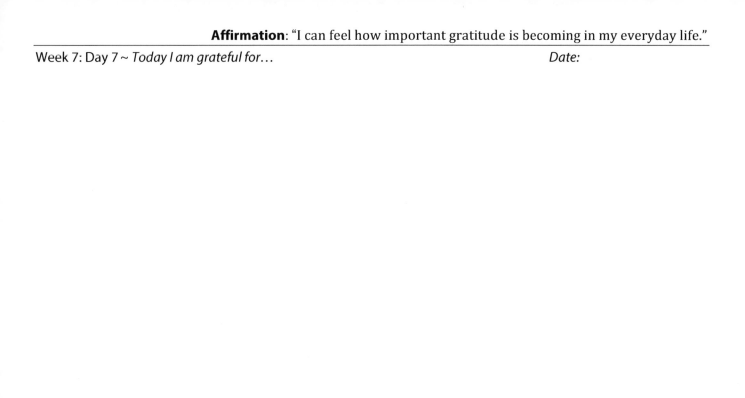

Week 8: Day 1 ~ *Today I am grateful for…*   *Date:*

Your week 8 podcast talks about how to keep going, even if you're secretly not in the mood. Discover why my favourite Sanskrit word – abhyasa – could be the key to your success.

Week 8: Day 2 ~ *Today I am grateful for…*   *Date:*

Really feel your gratitude. It's not about thinking. It's about letting 'thank you' fill every fibre of your being.

Affirmation: "I can feel how important gratitude is becoming in my everyday life."

Week 8: Day 3 ~ *Today I am grateful for…*   *Date:*

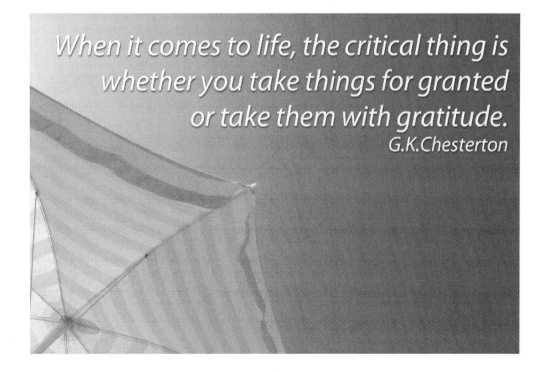

When it comes to life, the critical thing is whether you take things for granted or take them with gratitude.
G.K.Chesterton

Week 8: Day 4 ~ *Today I am grateful for…*   *Date:*

Week 8: Day 5 ~ *Today I am grateful for…*   *Date:*

Week 8: Day 6 ~ *Today I am grateful for…* Date:

Week 8: Day 7 ~ *Today I am grateful for…* Date:

Give yourself time to make these shifts. You wouldn't go for a single jog and expect to win the Olympics. Change takes time – and that's ok.

Make A Daily Date With A Gratitude Story

This time we're looking at the power of the Monkey Mind – your thinking mind - and its addiction to story-telling; specifically the stories we tell ourselves.

Don't believe every story your mind tells you.

One of the things I have found with one-to-one clients and seminar students over the past 15 years is that they're all at least as good as I am at telling themselves stories. We have all spent years, training our minds to evaluate, discuss, critique, re-tell, 'what-if', rehearse and even embellish stories about what goes on in life.

It's not the experience that hurts; it's the story we tell ourselves about it.

These stories often run in the background, half-unnoticed, while we're doing other things. But they're still there. The problem with the stories is that, whether you experience the event for real or just tell yourself a story about it, those thoughts trigger the same shifts in your body's chemistry and emotions, as though the event were really happening.

Your body can't tell the difference between what is 'here' and your mind's stories. It treats them all as real.

So if we tell ourselves an angry story, we get angry sensations in our body and feel angry emotions. Tell yourself a happy story and your auto-pilot happy hormones are released, triggering the physical and emotional experience of happiness for you.

With this next gratitude technique, you can experiment with deliberately using this auto-pilot response, to shift our experience of life. It's really simple. And it works! It's a great way to tame and retrain your Monkey Mind to concentrate on gratitude, rather than complaining.

Make A Daily Date With A Gratitude Story

1. **Deliberately choose a time, each day this week, to play with this technique.**
   Set an alarm. Do whatever it takes to make sure you keep that date. It only takes a few minutes, and setting a definite time means it will happen. Leaving it to chance means it probably won't.

2. **Take a 'snapshot'.**
   Pause for a moment and notice how you're feeling - physically and emotionally. Notice what your thoughts are. Notice the current tone of voice in your head.

3. **Think about an event that has happened (any time!) which triggers grateful emotions for you.**
Really allow yourself to dive into that experience. Feel the emotions you were feeling. Think the thoughts you were thinking. Hear the subtleties of the voice in your head shift. Notice the change in colour and vibrancy of any images you are seeing. Smile!

4. **Now for the fun! Imagine you are telling this story to someone else.**
Talk your way through the story, in your head (or out loud, if you have a willing audience!). Really help your story come to life. Share all the best bits. If it helps you dive into it, turn up the dial a few notches. *For this exercise, it doesn't matter if you embellish a little. It's about getting into the habit of shifting the tone of our stories.*

5. **When you feel you have finished, smile and thank yourself for taking the time.**
Repeat your 'snapshot' from step 2.
How have things changed? What did you notice? Can you sense a shift?

I'd love to hear how you get on with this strategy – there's a discussion thread waiting in the readers' club forum for you. Not joined yet? It's free: **www.ClareJosa.com/GratitudeClub**

Affirmation:
I choose to tell myself stories that make me smile.

Week 9: Day 1 ~ *Today I am grateful for…*   *Date:*

 Your week 9 podcast goes into more detail about how the stories we tell ourselves become the boxes within which we live – the well-defended walls of our comfort zones – plus you'll discover my 'magic wand' question for choosing a different story.

Affirmation: "I choose to tell myself stories that make me smile."

Week 9: Day 2 ~ *Today I am grateful for…*   *Date:*

Week 9: Day 3 ~ *Today I am grateful for…*   *Date:*

Affirmation:** "I choose to tell myself stories that make me smile."

Week 9: Day 4 ~ *Today I am grateful for…*   Date:

Week 9: Day 5 ~ *Today I am grateful for…*   Date:

"Some people grumble that roses have thorns. I am grateful that thorns have roses." - Alphonse Karr

53

Week 9: Day 6 ~ *Today I am grateful for…* *Date:*

Week 9: Day 7 ~ *Today I am grateful for…* *Date:*

"Thank you," she said and her heart fluttered with the joy of a butterfly on a spring breeze.

Week 10: Day 1 ~ *Today I am grateful for…*   *Date:*

 Continuing last week's theme, your week 10 podcast is all about the mind-body link – how the stories we tell ourselves affect every cell in our bodies and there's a simple technique that will prove it to you! Plus we're talking about how to get off the 'complaining train' and even ditch gossip-addiction!

Week 10: Day 2 ~ *Today I am grateful for…*   *Date:*

Affirmation: "I choose to tell myself stories that make me smile."

Week 10: Day 3 ~ *Today I am grateful for…*   *Date:*

Week 10: Day 4 ~ *Today I am grateful for…*   *Date:*

That which we can imagine, we can create. How about imagining a life filled with gratitude?

Week 10: Day 5 ~ *Today I am grateful for…*   *Date:*

Week 10: Day 6 ~ *Today I am grateful for…*   *Date:*

Affirmation: "I choose to tell myself stories that make me smile."

Week 10: Day 7 ~ *Today I am grateful for…*   *Date:*

 Pause for a moment to take a snapshot (see page 12). You can use this space to make any notes. And I'd love to hear how you're getting on, over at the readers' club discussion forum.

Are You Making The #1 Gratitude Mistake?

I'm curious: are you making what could be the number one mistake, when it comes to gratitude?
How can you tell if you're doing it? The gratitude techniques won't work as well for you – even the Gratitude Minutes might feel tough.

It's such a simple mistake that most of us don't even spot ourselves doing it – whether it's about gratitude or any other area of our lives. It's a habit. What is it?

Forcing yourself to do the techniques.

Of course, there's an argument that will power is an essential part of cultivating any new habit. But gratitude is about opening your heart to experiencing beautiful emotions – and sending those emotions out into the world. 'Forcing' tends to make your heart close, instead of opening.

Gritted teeth do not an open heart make…

Any time you do your gratitude practice with a mindset of "I have to" or "I should", you'll be creating the physiological changes in your body and mind that put you into your stress state.; feeding resistance. And saying "thank you" through clenched teeth is a very different experience to genuinely choosing to feel it.

What can you do instead?

It comes back to choosing. *Choose* to **play** with your gratitude techniques. *Choose* to **experiment** with them. Never force yourself. Do them with a light heart.

Even the simple thought of "*I choose to do this right now,*" will shift you back into re-balancing your parasympathetic nervous system (the relaxed bit) so that the sympathetic nervous system (the 'fight or flight' adrenalin-junky bit) is no longer running the show. And it makes it easier to smile.

When we are feeling relaxed, it is so much easier to open up your heart to experiencing gratitude, love, joy, happiness, inspiration and all the other wonderful emotions that Gratitude brings with it.

 Has "I have to" been sneaking into your practice at all? Or anywhere else in your life? How about letting it go and playing with "I choose to" today? There is a bonus article on this topic at the Readers' Club: www.ClareJosa.com/GratitudeClub And make sure you listen to this week's podcast episode!

Affirmation:
I set myself free from 'should' and 'have to'. I can always 'choose', instead

Week 11: Day 1 ~ *Today I am grateful for...*   *Date:*

Your week 11 podcast is all about how to set yourself free from 'shoulditis' – the secret epidemic.

Week 11: Day 2 ~ *Today I am grateful for...*   *Date:*

Week 11: Day 3 ~ *Today I am grateful for…*   *Date:*

Week 11: Day 4 ~ *Today I am grateful for…*   *Date:*

 Do you ever find it hard to make time for your Gratitude Minutes or other techniques? There's a bonus video on how to figure out what your gratitude excuses might be – and what you can do about them – over at the readers' club under the week 11 tab.

Affirmation: "I set myself free from 'should' and 'have to'. I can always 'choose', instead."

Week 11: Day 5 ~ *Today I am grateful for…*   *Date:*

Week 11: Day 6 ~ *Today I am grateful for…*   *Date:*

Affirmation: "I set myself free from 'should' and 'have to'. I can always 'choose', instead."

Week 11: Day 7 ~ *Today I am grateful for...*   *Date:*

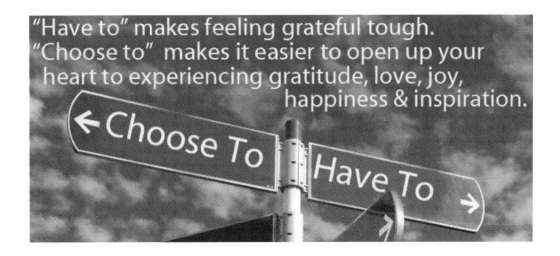

Week 12: Day 1 ~ *Today I am grateful for…*   *Date:*

In the week 12 podcast we're talking about our excuses – sorry – the legitimate reasons why we can't create the life we're secretly dreaming of. Hint: it's closely linked to 'shoulditis'. And it doesn't have to be that way.

Week 12: Day 2 ~ *Today I am grateful for…*   *Date:*

Week 12: Day 3 ~ *Today I am grateful for...*   *Date:*

Week 12: Day 4 ~ *Today I am grateful for...*   *Date:*

Week 12: Day 5 ~ *Today I am grateful for…*   *Date:*

Week 12: Day 6 ~ *Today I am grateful for…*   *Date:*

No matter what life throws at you, you can always choose to find a chink of gratitude, somewhere. And that will help you turn things around. The more you practise, the easier it is.

Week 12: Day 7 ~ *Today I am grateful for…*   *Date:*

I'd Love To Hear From You!
How have the techniques and practices in this journal been helping you so far? Do you have any questions? Any insights? Do you need some moral support? Could you offer some to others? I'd love to hear from you over at the readers' club forum.

Here's some space to make notes on the questions above.

How To Let Your 'To Do' List Change Your Life

How often do we begrudge day-to-day tasks?

How often do we do things with a heavy heart? With a sense of resentment? And how does it feel when we do it that way? Do we enjoy it? Does it feel good? Or does it cause us to grit our teeth and grumble our way through?

We all have the same number of minutes in a day. And, within reason, we have a huge amount of choice over how we spend them. The whole concept of 'have to' and 'not enough time' is a story concocted by the good old Monkey Mind, based on the diet we have fed it over the decades. The simple act of choosing, instead of feeling obligated, sets you free to experience that everyday task in a revolutionary way.

Add in some gratitude and, instead of being a burden, it becomes a path to freedom.

Instead of feeling grumpy about the task, you can work with it to come back to the present moment, to regain perspective, to practise gratitude and - surprisingly - even to recharge your batteries!

Feeling Gratitude For Everyday Tasks

We're building on the last technique and taking it to the next level. I invite you to pick an everyday task that bugs you a bit. That way you'll experience the shift this technique creates even more clearly. Choose something you'll do a number of times this week.

1. Start by remembering some of the recent times that you have done this task. Remember how it felt. Remember the kinds of thoughts you were thinking, while you are doing it. Remember how your body was feeling, physically, while you're doing it. Where was it holding tension?

2. Now do that task, but instead of feeling obligated, start by saying to yourself: I **choose** to do this.

3. As you carry out the task, wear a gentle smile on your lips, soften your jaw and eyes / eyebrows and, each time an irritated or grumpy thought comes up, say a silent "Thank you."

4. You might find it helps to use the 'thank you' mantra slowly throughout the task.

5. Allow yourself to be fully present and aware, experiencing the task with all of your senses. Do a great job of it.

6. When you have finished, pause and say a heart-felt "thank you" to yourself, for having completed the task.

How different did that feel? Let it build up over the weeks, rather than analysing it too much. The main thing is to allow yourself to be aware of the shifts that gratitude and acceptance are creating.

Affirmation:

I choose to enjoy the stuff that used to bug me on my 'to do' list.

Week 13: Day 1 ~ *Today I am grateful for…*   *Date:*

 In your week 13 podcast you'll discover the simple word-swap that shifts 'have to' into a genuine experience of gratitude, taking this week's technique to the next level. It's mind-blowingly effective.

Week 13: Day 2 ~ *Today I am grateful for…*   *Date:*

Week 13: Day 3 ~ *Today I am grateful for...*   *Date:*

Week 13: Day 4 ~ *Today I am grateful for...*   *Date:*

Gratitude can turn routine tasks into a chance to experience freedom.

Week 13: Day 5 ~ *Today I am grateful for…*   *Date:*

Week 13: Day 6 ~ *Today I am grateful for…*   *Date:*

Affirmation: "I choose to enjoy the stuff that used to bug me on my 'to do' list."

Week 13: Day 7 ~ *Today I am grateful for…*   *Date:*

Feeling grateful isn't an intellectual exercise; it impacts your body, mind and emotions, at every level.

Week 14: Day 1 ~ *Today I am grateful for...*   *Date:*

 In the week 14 podcast I'm giving you my 3Ds technique for cutting your 'to do' list in half, plus talking about why we so often say 'yes' when we are secretly screaming 'no'.

Week 14: Day 2 ~ *Today I am grateful for...*   *Date:*

Gratitude takes practice. It's a habit; not a magic wand!

Affirmation: "I choose to enjoy the stuff that used to bug me on my 'to do' list."

Week 14: Day 3 ~ *Today I am grateful for…*   *Date:*

Week 14: Day 4 ~ *Today I am grateful for…*   *Date:*

Week 14: Day 5 ~ *Today I am grateful for…*   *Date:*

Week 14: Day 6 ~ *Today I am grateful for…*   *Date:*

If you don't enjoy a task, don't do it! If that's not an option, how about choosing to enjoy it?

Week 14: Day 7 ~ *Today I am grateful for…*   *Date:*

 Pause for a moment to take a snapshot (see page 12). You can use this space to make any notes. And I'd love to hear how you're getting on, over at the readers' club forum.

Are You Trying Too Hard To Feel Grateful?

Are you leaping out of bed in the morning, excited about doing your gratitude practice? Or are you dragging yourself to it, because you feel you 'ought to' or 'have to' do it? Or are you *trying* to find time to do it, but it's not working out?

How many of us have fallen into the trap of trying, over and over again, to make something work? Remember the old proverb:

"If at first you don't succeed, try, try, try again."

There are two problems here:

- **Going Slightly Mad...**
  They say that doing the same thing over and over again, whilst expecting different results, is the one of the first signs of insanity. For most of us, "try, try, try again" involves just that...

- **"Trying" Gets Us Off The Hook.**
  When we use the word "try" – either out loud or in our heads – we're giving ourselves unconscious permission to fail. Think about it:
  *"I'll **try** to get that done by Tuesday."* Will it happen?
  *"I'll **try** harder to remember to do it next time."* Will it be different?

What Not To Do

If you are finding yourself struggling with some of your gratitude techniques, that's ok! You don't *have to* do them! I'm not suggesting you should give up or admit defeat. Just because your current approach hasn't been working doesn't mean there isn't one that will bring the results you're hoping for. That's why there are so many different techniques in this journal. Some you will love; some you won't. And that's ok.

What Can You Do Instead?

Do something different. If what you're doing isn't working, play with another approach. Focus on "what you want instead", rather than where you are now. Start telling a different story. Breaking the cycle could turn things around. And instead of the word "try", how about more encouraging and confident phrases like "I will..." or "I can..." or "I choose..." or – if you're not quite sure – "I hope..."

Gratitude isn't about 'doing' – it's about being. The more you let go of trying hard, the easier it will be to feel grateful.

Affirmation:

I choose to let go and 'be' grateful. I release trying too hard!

Week 15: Day 1 ~ *Today I am grateful for…*   *Date:*

In the week 15 podcast we're talking about 'force' vs 'flow' and how 'riding the waves and pulling out tent pegs' is my top advice for changing your life – and the world.

Week 15: Day 2 ~ *Today I am grateful for…*   *Date:*

Feeling grateful triggers chemical reactions that impact every cell in your body, promoting health, healing and happiness.

Week 15: Day 3 ~ *Today I am grateful for…*   *Date:*

Week 15: Day 4 ~ *Today I am grateful for…*   *Date:*

Week 15: Day 5 ~ *Today I am grateful for...*   *Date:*

Week 15: Day 6 ~ *Today I am grateful for...*   *Date:*

Let us rise up and be thankful, for if we didn't learn a lot today, at least we learned a little, and if we didn't learn a little, at least we didn't get sick, and if we got sick, at least we didn't die; so, let us all be thankful. - Buddha

Week 15: Day 7 ~ *Today I am grateful for...*   *Date:*

Week 16: Day 1 ~ *Today I am grateful for...*   *Date:*

 In the week 16 podcast we're talking about the dangers of 'doing your best' and how we can 'reparent' our inner child to feel accepted for who they really are.

Affirmation: "I choose to let go and 'be' grateful. I release trying too hard!"

Week 16: Day 2 ~ *Today I am grateful for…*   *Date:*

Week 16: Day 3 ~ *Today I am grateful for…*   *Date:*

Giving thanks for the good you already have opens the door to abundance in your life.

Week 16: Day 4 ~ *Today I am grateful for…*   *Date:*

Week 16: Day 5 ~ *Today I am grateful for…*   *Date:*

Affirmation: "I choose to let go and 'be' grateful. I release trying too hard!"

Week 16: Day 6 ~ *Today I am grateful for…*   *Date:*

Week 16: Day 7 ~ *Today I am grateful for…*   *Date:*

Every time you say 'thank you', you take another step
towards the life you have been dreaming of.

84

Gratitude For An Every-Day Object

Today I'd like to share with you a technique which is a truly potent way of bringing gratitude into your daily life, rather than saving it for the 'big stuff'. It opens your heart to a different way of seeing the world.

Here's how to do it:

1. Pick an every-day object – perhaps something you use several times a day, maybe a pen, your keys, your watch – whatever you see in front of you.

2. Hold the object in your hand and really 'see it' – I mean be 'present' with it, rather than half-looking at it, while talking to yourself about something else…

3. Become aware of its shape, its form, its colour, its texture, any sounds it makes, the way it feels in your hand. Allow yourself to notice the details that you perhaps haven't seen before.

4. Now gently allow your heart to soften as you say 'thank you' to this object. Thank it for the role it plays in your life. You don't have to 'tell a story' or get into details; simply the words 'thank you', said from the heart, are what are needed.

5. Continue until you feel the exercise is complete and release the practice, with a gentle smile on your face.

How did that feel? Can you imagine how life might shift if you did this for a few seconds with random objects throughout your day? How about giving it a go?

 Let us know which objects you choose and how this exercise feels, over at the readers' club forum!

Affirmation:
I choose to feel grateful for the things that help me through my day.

Practising feeling grateful for everyday objects will shift your experience of life faster than a magic wand!

Week 17: Day 1 ~ *Today I am grateful for…*   *Date:*

Your week 17 podcast is all about how looking after what you have already is the key to attracting more abundance into your life.

Week 17: Day 2 ~ *Today I am grateful for…*   *Date:*

"Piglet noticed that even though he had a Very Small Heart, it could hold a rather large amount of Gratitude." — A.A. Milne, Winnie-the-Pooh

Affirmation: "I choose to feel grateful for the things that help me through my day."

Week 17: Day 3 ~ *Today I am grateful for…*   *Date:*

Week 17: Day 4 ~ *Today I am grateful for…*   *Date:*

87

Affirmation: "I choose to feel grateful for the things that help me through my day."

Week 17: Day 5 ~ *Today I am grateful for…*   *Date:*

Week 17: Day 6 ~ *Today I am grateful for…*   *Date:*

Week 17: Day 7 ~ *Today I am grateful for...*   *Date:*

Do you ever wish you could get more support for your Gratitude Time? Remember your 'Big Why' from week 7? Tell it to those whose support you need!

"I choose to take time out for a few minutes a day to do my gratitude practices, because..."

The word *'**because**'* has an amazing power to get people to listen to your request and to help you. When they understand **why** you want their help and why you want them to support you, it makes it much easier for them to buy in. You might be surprised how much friends, family and co-workers do want to support you. Some of them might even want to join in with you.

The key is to decide when you are going to do all of this, where and what you need to clear out of the way to allow you to do that, and to remember why you're bothering.

There's a bonus video in the readers' club about how to get your family, friends and colleagues "Gratitude-Fit" – secrets to enlist their support. And remember, we're your virtual cheerleaders, too, over at the forum!

www.ClareJosa.com/GratitudeClub

Affirmation: "I choose to feel grateful for the things that help me through my day."

Week 18: Day 1 ~ *Today I am grateful for...*   *Date:*

In week 18's podcast you'll learn about the hidden power of the word 'because' to change your life, particularly if you struggle with boundaries or asking for what you need.

Week 18: Day 2 ~ *Today I am grateful for...*   *Date:*

Week 18: Day 3 ~ *Today I am grateful for…*   *Date:*

Week 18: Day 4 ~ *Today I am grateful for…*   *Date:*

"As we express our gratitude, we must never forget that the highest appreciation is not to utter words, but to live by them.." - John F. Kennedy

Affirmation: "I choose to feel grateful for the things that help me through my day."

Week 18: Day 5 ~ *Today I am grateful for...*   *Date:*

Week 18: Day 6 ~ *Today I am grateful for...*   *Date:*

Week 18: Day 7 ~ *Today I am grateful for…*   *Date:*

Pause for a moment to take a snapshot (see page 12). You can use this space to make any notes. I'd love to hear how you're getting on, over at the readers' club forum!

Taking Gratitude For That Every-Day Object To The Next Level

How have you been getting on with feeling gratitude for an every-day object? Today I invite you to take this to the next level, by giving gratitude to everyone who was involved with getting that object to you. It can be quite a transformational exercise.

1. Like last time, pick an every-day object – perhaps something you use several times a day, maybe a pen, your keys, your watch – whatever you see in front of you.

2. Hold the object in your hand and really 'see it'. Become aware of its shape, its form, its colour, its texture, any sounds it makes, the way it feels in your hand. Allow yourself to notice the details that you perhaps haven't seen before.

3. Now gently allow your heart to soften as you say 'thank you' to this object. Thank it for the role it plays in your life. You don't have to 'tell a story' or get into details; simply the words 'thank you', said from the heart, are what are needed.

4. Next start to imagine each person who was involved with helping that object to get to you – and say a silent 'thank you' to them:

    -   Somebody first imagined it – thank you
    -   Somebody had the idea to make it – thank you
    -   Somebody figured out how to make it – thank you
    -   Somebody set up the factory or workshop where it was made – thank you
    -   Somebody (or many people) physically made it – sourcing the raw materials, designing the machines and manufacturing processes and actually doing the 'making' – thank you
    -   Somebody decided to buy it, wholesale, and to stock it in their shop – thank you
    -   Somebody ran that shop and worked in that shop, so you could buy it – thank you.

5. Experience and feel how each person's actions helped you – a complete stranger whom you will, most likely, never meet. It doesn't matter whether or not it was their 'job'. They still helped you.

6. How does it shift your view of life?

This exercise helps you to look at everything around you through a lens of gratitude. It shifts our perspective and opens our heart and mind to seeing from the viewpoint of gratitude. That has a deep impact on even the cellular level processes in our bodies and can truly change our lives.

Affirmation:
I feel grateful for the people I have never met, but who have still helped me.

Week 19: Day 1 ~ *Today I am grateful for…*   *Date:*

In your week 19 podcast we're talking about three reasons why the locals thought I was weird when I lived in Germany – and how what I learned from this could clear one of your hidden gratitude blocks.

Week 19: Day 2 ~ *Today I am grateful for…*   *Date:*

Affirmation: "I feel grateful for the people I have never met, but who still help me."

Week 19: Day 3 ~ *Today I am grateful for…*   *Date:*

Week 19: Day 4 ~ *Today I am grateful for…*   *Date:*

"If the only prayer you said was thank you, that would be enough." — *Meister Eckhart.*

Week 19: Day 5 ~ *Today I am grateful for…*   *Date:*

Week 19: Day 6 ~ *Today I am grateful for…*   *Date:*

Affirmation: "I feel grateful for the people I have never met, but who still help me."

Week 19: Day 7 ~ *Today I am grateful for…*   Date:

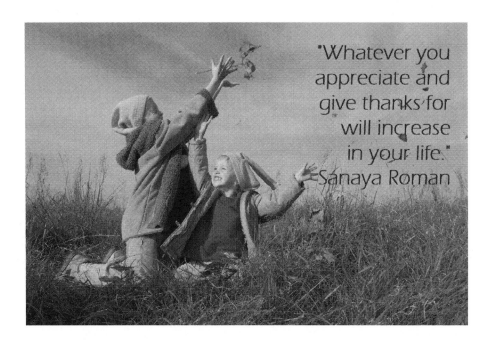

"Whatever you appreciate and give thanks for will increase in your life." —Sanaya Roman

Week 20: Day 1 ~ *Today I am grateful for…*   *Date:*

 In the week 20 podcast you'll find out how we accidentally hard-wire 'complaining' into our brain and how A Year Full Of Gratitude is rewiring things for you.

Week 20: Day 2 ~ *Today I am grateful for…*   *Date:*

Affirmation: "I feel grateful for the people I have never met, but who still help me."

Week 20: Day 3 ~ *Today I am grateful for...*   *Date:*

Week 20: Day 4 ~ *Today I am grateful for...*   *Date:*

Week 20: Day 5 ~ *Today I am grateful for…*   *Date:*

Week 20: Day 6 ~ *Today I am grateful for…*   *Date:*

When you look at the world through the lens of gratitude, the world you look at changes.

Affirmation: "I feel grateful for the people I have never met, but who still help me."

Week 20: Day 7 ~ *Today I am grateful for…*   *Date:*

Just wondering...

What kinds of shifts have you noticed so far?

How has gratitude helped you, over recent weeks?

How would you describe the benefits of working with A Year Full Of Gratitude, so far?

How about sharing your answers via the special discussion thread in the readers' club? And do you know any friends who might love to join you on your Year Full Of Gratitude journey?

My Favourite Way To 'Magically' Make More Time

"I don't have enough time!" It's a modern epidemic. People tell us to stop and relax, but there's never enough time. Or is there?

Today I'd like to share with you a near-magic-wand for creating more time in your day.
No, it's not a time machine. It's a single gratitude phrase. And its effects can feel miraculous.

How often do we spend our time fretting about not having enough time? It seems to fly by. And the more stressed we are, the faster it goes. **But time is largely a matter of perception.**

When we're hiding away in the realms of the Monkey Mind and its stories of stress, time is a scarce resource over which we have no control. We run the mantra, "I don't have enough time." And we're right.

In fact:

Whether you think you have enough time or you think you don't, you're right.

So how can you magically create the feeling of having more time?

By being grateful for the time you have.

Giving gratitude for the time you have lets go of the Monkey Mind's stress-stories and helps time to expand. You can think more clearly; you can de-stress; you can concentrate better; you fritter away less time with worries and Monkey Mind stories; you can have sudden flashes of insight. Life starts to flow. Time seems to expand.

So if you feel rushed and need more time, allow yourself to experience more time with the magical mantra:

I am grateful for the time I have.

After all, that's all the time we're ever going to get, so why on earth waste it by feeling grumpy about it?

Affirmation:
I am grateful for the time I have.

YOU HAVE THE GIFT OF 1,440 MINUTES TODAY. HAVE YOU USED ONE OF THEM TO SAY THANK YOU?

Affirmation: "I am grateful for the time I have."

Week 21: Day 1 ~ *Today I am grateful for…*   *Date:*

In the week 21 podcast we're talking about secret time thieves, the effect of feeling time-poor on your brain's performance and how "I don't have enough time!" becomes a self-fulfilling prophecy.

Week 21: Day 2 ~ *Today I am grateful for…*   *Date:*

Week 21: Day 3 ~ *Today I am grateful for…*   *Date:*

Week 21: Day 4 ~ *Today I am grateful for…*   *Date:*

It is not the years in your life but the life in your years
that counts.. - Adlai Stevenson

Affirmation: "I am grateful for the time I have."

Week 21: Day 5 ~ *Today I am grateful for…*   *Date:*

Week 21: Day 6 ~ *Today I am grateful for…*   *Date:*

To show true gratitude to your blessings, it's important not just to count them, but to make them count.

Week 21: Day 7 ~ *Today I am grateful for…*   *Date:*

Week 22: Day 1 ~ *Today I am grateful for…*   *Date:*

 In the week 22 podcast we're diving in to self-doubt – how counting your blessings can crank up your confidence without feeling you're being arrogant.

Affirmation: "I am grateful for the time I have."

Week 22: Day 2 ~ *Today I am grateful for…*   *Date:*

Week 22: Day 3 ~ *Today I am grateful for…*   *Date:*

Affirmation: "I am grateful for the time I have."

Week 22: Day 4 ~ *Today I am grateful for...*   *Date:*

Week 22: Day 5 ~ *Today I am grateful for...*   *Date:*

Being consciously grateful for the gifts life has given you helps you to feel
really alive – and blessed!

Affirmation: "I am grateful for the time I have."

Week 22: Day 6 ~ *Today I am grateful for…*   *Date:*

Week 22: Day 7 ~ *Today I am grateful for…*   *Date:*

Pause for a moment to take a snapshot (see page 12). You can use this space to make any notes. I'd love to hear how you're getting on, over at the readers' club forum.

Could You Become A Grateful Consumer?

What do I mean by 'consume'? I'm talking about everything that we use or take in, in our daily lives. That can include:

•   Food – that one's obvious
•   Water – drinking, washing, cleaning, bathing, gardening
•   Fuel – heating our homes and fuelling our cars, buses and trains, cooking our food
•   The internet – the many thousands of words that most of us read each day
•   Newspapers & magazines
•   TV & radio

And this is just the beginning of the list.

Most of us consume, consume, consume, without giving it a second thought. We're often completely unaware of what we're 'consuming'. By pausing every now and then to notice what 'goes in', we can become more aware of its impact on us, at a deeper level, then choosing whether or not to continue to consume it.

Then, by giving gratitude for that which we consciously consume, we are connecting with that element of life at a heart-centred level, transforming our experience of it. [… *continues*]

That might not make sense yet, but by the end of the next few weeks, you'll know what I mean with this! I'd like to share a mind-shifting quote from Einstein:

There are only two ways to live your life. One is that nothing is a miracle; the other is as though everything is a miracle.

And you don't have to be a genius to figure out which of those options we're choosing today!

When we experience life through the filter of everything being mundane, it triggers that pesky old 'have to' response, where we live from the point of view of everything feeling like an obligation. In that world, we have to **make** everything happen – there is no space for magic, wonder, miracles, inspiration or spontaneity.

When we choose to experience life through the filter of everything being a miracle, then imagine how that opens your heart and mind up to the wonder of life! Imagine how that might affect your relationship with others! And yourself?

My invitation to you for the next few weeks (and beyond!) is to become a 'Conscious Consumer' of everything (within reason!) in life. And to consume it with gratitude.

Want to give it a go?

Our next gratitude technique guides you through turning something that we often take for granted into a deep experience of gratitude.

It's all about food. And saying thank you for it – but in a slightly different way to the old mumbled-grace of school canteen days. I invite you to play with it, perhaps each mealtime this week, and notice the shifts it helps you to create.

1. When you sit down to eat, actually look at the food on your plate (it's amazing how often we don't!)
2. Pause for a moment and connect with the part of you that wakes up when you do your gratitude practices.
3. Look at your food and say a heart-felt 'thank you'. Do this three times. Then start to eat.
4. If this resonates for you, you might want to experiment with saying 'thank you' as you lift your fork and put your food in your mouth.
5. The easiest way to try this, the first few times, is with a quiet meal, where you can be 'present' and give it your attention, so perhaps turn the radio or TV off and maybe even tell anyone you're eating what you're doing, so they will give you the space to enjoy this experience.

Affirmation:

I choose to experience life as being full of miracles.

Week 23: Day 1 ~ *Today I am grateful for…*   *Date:*

 In the week 23 podcast I share a gratitude-twist on the classic 'raisin mindfulness' technique. Plus we're talking about where 'miracles' come from!

Week 23: Day 2 ~ *Today I am grateful for…*   *Date:*

"The moment one gives close attention to anything, even a blade of grass, it becomes a mysterious, awesome, indescribably magnificent world in itself." - Henry Miller

Week 23: Day 3 ~ *Today I am grateful for…*   *Date:*

Week 23: Day 4 ~ *Today I am grateful for…*   *Date:*

Week 23: Day 5 ~ *Today I am grateful for…*   *Date:*

Week 23: Day 6 ~ *Today I am grateful for…*   *Date:*

Affirmation: "I choose to experience life as being full of miracles."

Week 23: Day 7 ~ *Today I am grateful for…*   *Date:*

Week 24: Day 1 ~ *Today I am grateful for…*   *Date:*

 In the week 24 podcast you'll learn how to become a miracle-finder, why this transforms your experience of life and how it gives your inner critic a loving, but firm, wet-kipper slap.

Week 24: Day 2 ~ *Today I am grateful for…*   *Date:*

Week 24: Day 3 ~ *Today I am grateful for…*   *Date:*

When you look for miracles in your every-day life, you'll find them. If you don't, you won't.

Affirmation: "I choose to experience life as being full of miracles."

Week 24: Day 4 ~ *Today I am grateful for…*   *Date:*

Week 24: Day 5 ~ *Today I am grateful for…*   *Date:*

"Enough is a feast." – Buddhist proverb

Week 24: Day 6 ~ *Today I am grateful for…*   *Date:*

Week 24: Day 7 ~ *Today I am grateful for…*   *Date:*

What Colour Are Your Glasses?

We have all heard about wearing rose-tinted glasses, but we usually dismiss them as being only for the Pollyanna brigade. Instead, we'd rather wallow around with our black glasses on, telling ourselves stories of how awful things are. Or would we?

When you view life through the lens of gratitude, the world you see changes. But how do you get your glasses to be gratitude-coloured, when you're having to deal with the problems and challenges in 'real' life?

Letting gratitude help you with your problems

1. Take a situation that you would currently call a 'problem'. Make it a 2-3 out of 10, rather than a 200/10!

2. Take a 'snapshot': when you think about that situation, how does it feel in your physical body? Emotionally? What kinds of thoughts are you thinking?

3. Whatever is going on, whoever is saying or doing stuff to annoy you, put that on hold for the next few moments. Press pause on the story. You can choose whether or not to pick it back up when we're done.

4. Ask yourself – and be really open-hearted and honest about this –
   *"What's **true** in this?" cut out the drama-story and then "What in this situation could I choose to feel grateful for?" Please feel free to lob rotten tomatoes at me, if it helps. But I'm going to keep gently and firmly pressing this button until you have an answer!* Chances are there will be something – even if it's really small.

5. Now let the feeling of gratitude for that aspect gently grow. Feel the subtle sense of relief, as you let your focus rest on that aspect for which you could choose to feel grateful.

6. Now ask yourself – open-heartedly, again –
   "What else in this situation could I choose to feel grateful for?"
   Again, let that feeling of gratitude gently grow. Feel and enjoy the relief it brings.

7. Keep going with this process until you have found at least 3 things (ideally more) to feel grateful for in the situation. Really let those gentle waves of gratitude wash through you and the situation.

8. Now, going back to the 'problem', how does it feel now? How has it shifted?

How might this technique help you in daily life? How different would things look, if you chose to view them through the filter of love and gratitude and hope? There's a special discussion thread in our readers' club forum.

Affirmation:
I choose to put on my gratitude-coloured glasses today.

Week 25: Day 1 ~ *Today I am grateful for…*   *Date:*

 In the week 25 podcast we're diving back into neuroscience, learning how the stories we tell ourselves create our limiting beliefs – and how gratitude can near-effortlessly reprogramme them.

Week 25: Day 2 ~ *Today I am grateful for…*   *Date:*

Affirmation: "I choose to put on my gratitude-glasses today"

Week 25: Day 3 ~ *Today I am grateful for…*   *Date:*

Week 25: Day 4 ~ *Today I am grateful for…*   *Date:*

If you look for the good in life, you will find it.

Week 25: Day 5 ~ *Today I am grateful for...*   *Date:*

Week 25: Day 6 ~ *Today I am grateful for...*   *Date:*

Affirmation: "I choose to put on my gratitude-glasses today"

Week 25: Day 7 ~ *Today I am grateful for…*   *Date:*

Week 26: Day 1 ~ *Today I am grateful for…*   *Date:*

 In your week 26 podcast you'll find out why 'can' is not the opposite of 'can't' and what you can use, instead, if you're creating your own positive affirmations.

Week 26: Day 2 ~ *Today I am grateful for…*   *Date:*

Week 26: Day 3 ~ *Today I am grateful for…*   *Date:*

If you are not grateful for what you already have, then how will getting more make you happy?

Week 26: Day 4 ~ *Today I am grateful for...*   *Date:*

Week 26: Day 5 ~ *Today I am grateful for...*   *Date:*

"The struggle ends when the gratitude begins.." - Neale Donald Walsch

Week 26: Day 6 ~ *Today I am grateful for…*   *Date:*

Week 26: Day 7 ~ *Today I am grateful for…*   *Date:*

Thank You Everyone, For Everything

Today I'd like to share with you a simple Chinese proverb, which helps to illustrate the power of connecting with others from the heart:

"When eating bamboo sprouts, remember the person who planted them."

Every object in our experience of life is there because of the efforts of someone else. In fact, most of our experiences in life, not just the objects, have been dependent on the efforts of someone else.

When you experience life from that perspective, suddenly the Universe feels like a truly kind and generous place. And it becomes easier to feel blessed – and full of gratitude.

I'm curious: what have you been doing today that will impact the lives of others? How could you shift your mindset to help you to view your actions as spreading kindness and gratitude throughout your world? Even at work?

How does that impact how you're feeling, right now?

Affirmation:

I choose to experience myself as spreading kindness and gratitude, with each and every action.

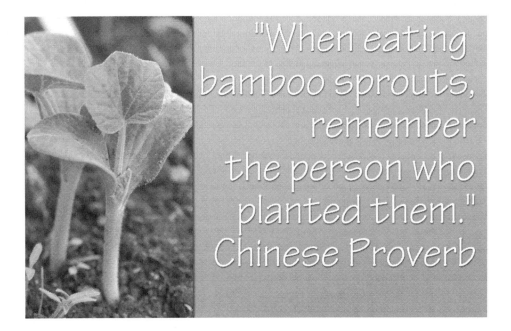

Affirmation: "I choose to experience myself as spreading kindness and gratitude, with each and every action."

Week 27: Day 1 ~ *Today I am grateful for...*   *Date:*

In your week 27 podcast you'll learn why planting seeds of kindness can rewrite your personal history.

Week 27: Day 2 ~ *Today I am grateful for...*   *Date:*

Week 27: Day 3 ~ *Today I am grateful for...*   *Date:*

Week 27: Day 4 ~ *Today I am grateful for...*   *Date:*

"I challenge anybody in their darkest moment to write what they're grateful for, even stupid little things like green grass or a friendly conversation on the elevator. You start to realize how rich you are." - Jim Carrey

Week 27: Day 5 ~ *Today I am grateful for…*   *Date:*

Week 27: Day 6 ~ *Today I am grateful for…*   *Date:*

Affirmation: "I choose to experience myself as spreading kindness and gratitude, with each and every action."

Week 27: Day 7 ~ *Today I am grateful for…*   *Date:*

 Pause for a moment to take a snapshot (see page 12). You can use this space to make any notes. I'd love to hear how you're getting on so far – you can let me know over at the readers' forum.

Week 28: Day 1 ~ *Today I am grateful for…*   *Date:*

Your week 28 podcast covers one of my favourite topics: 'secondary gain' – in other words what keeps us stuck doing that crazy habit we want to ditch. It's the secret to near-zero-effort life-change.

Week 28: Day 23 ~ *Today I am grateful for…*   *Date:*

Saying 'thank you' to someone could make their day – or even change their life. Sure that's worth a moment of your time today?

Week 28: Day 3 ~ *Today I am grateful for…*   *Date:*

Week 28: Day 4 ~ *Today I am grateful for…*   *Date:*

We tend to get what we think about. If you think about what's wrong, you'll spot more of it. If you think about feeling grateful, you'll find even more reasons to say 'thank you'.

Week 28: Day 5 ~ *Today I am grateful for…*   *Date:*

Week 28: Day 6 ~ *Today I am grateful for…*   *Date:*

Affirmation: "I choose to experience myself as spreading kindness and gratitude, with each and every action."

Week 28: Day 7 ~ *Today I am grateful for…*   *Date:*

Want to change your life?
By all means keep playing with the techniques you enjoy,
but the
real gifts lie in those
that you have been resisting.

There's a bonus video on this waiting for you over at the readers' club (under the Week 28 tab.

In the forum we're talking about why we resist change and strategies for getting to the other side, without having to 'push on through the pain barrier' or 'feel the fear and do it anyway'.

Let's Talk About Self-Doubt…

"I'm not [fill in the blank] enough!"

Self-doubt sneaks in as a secret 3am fear. Even the nation's board rooms are full of people struggling with Imposter Syndrome – "Who am *I* to…?" So you're in great company. But you're also the only person with the power to turn this around – and gratitude can help. As Eleanor Roosevelt said:

No one can make you feel inferior without your consent.

But the person normally making us feel less-than-worthy is usually us. Yes, that inner voice may have someone else's tone, but we're the ones telling ourselves that story.

So your exercise for this week is to make your gratitude minutes and journal entries about yourself – things you are doing well; things you can appreciate about yourself; thanking the 'younger you' for things they achieved.

I know this can feel tough, so let's take this one minute at a time. And let me know what shifts, over at the readers' club forum.

Affirmation:
It's time to let my light shine.

Week 29: Day 1 ~ Today I am grateful for…   Date:

 Your week 29 podcast guides you through the two types of fear and why only one of them deserves our attention – and how to spot if this is keeping you stuck, dreaming big but playing small.

Week 29: Day 2 ~ *Today I am grateful for...*   *Date:*

Week 29: Day 3 ~ *Today I am grateful for...*   *Date:*

Week 29: Day 4 ~ *Today I am grateful for…*   *Date:*

Week 29: Day 5 ~ *Today I am grateful for…*   *Date:*

No matter how dark the rain clouds, there is
always something to be thankful for.

139

Affirmation: "It's time to let my light shine."

Week 29: Day 6 ~ *Today I am grateful for…*   *Date:*

Week 29: Day 7 ~ *Today I am grateful for…*   *Date:*

Gratitude puts a smile on your face, much more easily than grumbling ever could.

Week 30: Day 1 ~ *Today I am grateful for…*   *Date:*

 Your week 30 podcast takes another look at self-talk. Now you know what you know, how can you shift it to help you feel more confident, without feeling cocky?

Week 30: Day 2 ~ *Today I am grateful for…*   *Date:*

Affirmation: "It's time to let my light shine."

Week 30: Day 3 ~ *Today I am grateful for…*   *Date:*

Week 30: Day 4 ~ *Today I am grateful for…*   *Date:*

Week 30: Day 5 ~ *Today I am grateful for…*   *Date:*

Week 30: Day 6 ~ *Today I am grateful for…*   *Date:*

"Gratitude to gratitude always gives birth." – Sophocles

Pause for a moment to take a snapshot (see page 12). You can use this space to make any notes. I'd love to hear how you're getting on, over at the readers' club forum!

Feeling Gratitude For Those You Love

How often do we actually pause to say 'thank you' to those we love? It's funny how those we appreciate the most are the ones who often feel taken for granted. We rarely take time out to thank them – either in their presence or in our hearts.

"But of course I appreciate you!" is heard more often in the marriage counsellor's office than in the home.

So for the next gratitude technique, I'm inviting you to spend some time really becoming aware of the people in your life for whom you feel grateful. Take some quiet time to focus on them, one by one, saying a heart-felt 'thank you', as you imagine them in front of you.

Notice how sometimes this can make our fears of rejection and old hurts come up – sometimes we feel the need to wear our invisible armour – and that's ok. Being aware of all of this is an important first step. Accept it and perhaps notice that you can let your guard drop, when you connect from your heart. But there's no rush.

When you have played with this technique in your heart, it's so much easier to connect with those you love from a place of gratitude, out in the 'real world'.

Affirmation:
I send love and gratitude to the people in my life.

Week 31: Day 1 ~ *Today I am grateful for…*   *Date:*

 Your week 31 podcast is about how to gain the benefit of hindsight from the 'future you'. It's as close as we're likely to get to time-travelling at the moment and it can be transformational.

Affirmation: "I send love and gratitude to the people in my life."

Week 31: Day 2 ~ *Today I am grateful for...*   *Date:*

Week 31: Day 3 ~ *Today I am grateful for...*   *Date:*

Affirmation: "I send love and gratitude to the people in my life."

Week 31: Day 4 ~ *Today I am grateful for…*   *Date:*

Week 31: Day 5 ~ *Today I am grateful for…*   *Date:*

Consciously choosing to think of things you feel happy about or grateful for is one of the most effective ways to re-programme your thought habits.

Affirmation: "I send love and gratitude to the people in my life."

Week 31: Day 6 ~ *Today I am grateful for…*   *Date:*

Week 31: Day 7 ~ *Today I am grateful for…*   *Date:*

It is often only by looking back that we see the clear path to the future. Your gratitude journal is a powerful shortcut.

Affirmation: "I send love and gratitude to the people in my life."

Week 32: Day 1 ~ *Today I am grateful for…*   *Date:*

 Your week 32 podcast brings you my favourite magic wand for worrying. You won't want to miss this!

Week 32: Day 2 ~ *Today I am grateful for…*   *Date:*

Affirmation: "I send love and gratitude to the people in my life."

Week 32: Day 3 ~ *Today I am grateful for…*   *Date:*

Week 32: Day 4 ~ *Today I am grateful for…*   *Date:*

Week 32: Day 5 ~ *Today I am grateful for…*   *Date:*

Week 32: Day 6 ~ *Today I am grateful for…*   *Date:*

It's easy to think grateful thoughts about that for which you feel grateful. But the real gift of freedom comes in feeling gratitude towards that for which you're not yet grateful!

Affirmation: "I send love and gratitude to the people in my life."

Week 32: Day 7 ~ *Today I am grateful for…*   *Date:*

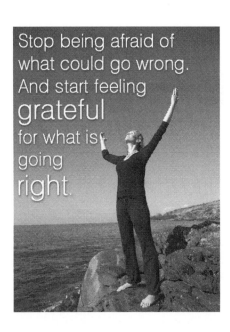

Stop being afraid of what could go wrong. And start feeling grateful for what is going right.

Giving Gratitude For Those Who Bug You!

It's fairly easy to feel grateful for those we love – for those who are kind to us.

The real challenge is feeling grateful for those who bug us!

"She's gone mad!" I can hear you yell…

But true inner peace comes from being able to feel love and acceptance and gratitude towards everyone in our experience. It's not about pretending that everything is ok. It's about accepting that the person who is bugging you is deserving of your compassion.

> *"All criticism comes of someone else's pain."* ~ *Native American saying*

If that 'buggy' person were feeling happy, they would be unlikely to behave in a way that was unkind or annoying. Happy people don't hurt others.

> *There is a story about Buddha being confronted by an angry man, shouting at Buddha and behaving very rudely and unkindly. Instead of retaliating, Buddha asked the man, "If you buy someone a gift and they won't accept it, to whom does the gift belong?"*
>
> *The man replied that it would still be his gift, of course, because he had bought it. Buddha responded by telling the man that he was correct. And that it was the same with the man's anger. If the man tried to give Buddha his anger, but Buddha chose not to accept it, instead treating the man with compassion, the anger still belonged to the man. So the man was just hurting himself.*

Until we can let go of our needs to retaliate, to hurt, to win arguments and to behave unkindly in response to unkind behaviour, we will continue to hurt ourselves; to feel pain in our hearts.

If we can cultivate compassion towards others, through exercises such as feeling gratitude for their 'good bits' (most people have plenty of these, if we're honest with ourselves!), we can set ourselves free from the old pain cycle. And the other person no longer has power over how we feel.

So, for the next few weeks, I invite you to think of people who bug you (play with this at the 3 out of 10 level – not those who drive you crazy!) and consciously choose to see things in them for which you can feel gratitude. I promise you, it will change your life.

Affirmation:

I choose to find things to feel grateful about in everyone I meet – even those who might bug me.

Week 33: Day 1 ~ *Today I am grateful for…*   *Date:*

Your week 33 podcast is about dealing with difficult people – without totally losing your rag.

Week 33: Day 2 ~ *Today I am grateful for…*   *Date:*

154

Week 33: Day 3 ~ *Today I am grateful for…*   *Date:*

Week 33: Day 4 ~ *Today I am grateful for…*   *Date:*

It is easy to love a rose, but it takes effort to appreciate its thorns.

Affirmation: "I choose to find things to feel grateful about in everyone I meet – even those who might bug me."

Week 33: Day 5 ~ *Today I am grateful for…*   *Date:*

Week 33: Day 6 ~ *Today I am grateful for…*   *Date:*

Look for the good in people and you will find it is there, waiting for you.

Week 33: Day 7 ~ *Today I am grateful for…*   *Date:*

Week 34: Day 1 ~ *Today I am grateful for…*   *Date:*

 The week 34 podcast is about how to handle energy vampires, without resorting to wooden stakes or necklaces of garlic.

Week 34: Day 2 ~ *Today I am grateful for...*   *Date:*

Week 34: Day 3 ~ *Today I am grateful for...*   *Date:*

Affirmation: "I choose to find things to feel grateful about in everyone I meet – even those who might bug me."

Week 34: Day 4 ~ *Today I am grateful for…*   *Date:*

Week 34: Day 5 ~ *Today I am grateful for…*   *Date:*

Express your gratitude! Keep it to yourself and it might change your life;
share it and it might change the world.

Affirmation: "I choose to find things to feel grateful about in everyone I meet – even those who might bug me."

Week 34: Day 6 ~ *Today I am grateful for…*   *Date:*

Week 34: Day 7 ~ *Today I am grateful for…*   *Date:*

Want to share how you are getting on with this? Let me know over at the readers' club forum.

What Are Your Body-Story Habits?

Today we're moving on to the body! We're going to dive in and discover the transformations that gratitude can create for you in the way you think about your body, how it feels and even how it looks.

I'd like to start by inviting you to spot the stories you are currently telling yourself about your body:

> *When you think about your body, what's the first thing that comes to mind…? And the next thing…? And the next thing…?*

Chances are you weren't telling yourself stories about how amazing your body is. Most of us spend much more time complaining about our bodies than feeling grateful for them.

Telling yourself negative stories about your body – everything it can't do and all of its aches and pains – makes it really hard for you to appreciate your body; to feel gratitude towards it. But 'telling it off' and complaining about it saps your energy and makes it hard for you to feel vibrant and healthy.

If you tell yourself that you're feeling tired or unwell, that's what you will experience. (There's a quick game to prove this to you, over at the free Readers' Club on the Week 35 tab.

Do you really want to beat yourself up about your body? Or would you like to feel good about it?

The way you feel about your body is a habit, not a truth.

And gratitude can turn things around, if you want it to.

Thoughts trigger the biochemical reactions in the body that impact our emotions and behaviours. So if you want to change your outside (or even get ok with your 'outside'!), then you need to change your 'inside' – your thoughts and beliefs about your body. After all, your body has got you this far, so it can't be that bad, can it?

If you want to shift how you're feeling about your body – and experience the transformation this can create in other areas of your life, then it's time for our old friend, gratitude! Instead of telling yourself stories about what your body ***can't*** do, it's time retrain your Monkey Mind to tell your stories about what it ***can*** do. And that's the whole point of this week's gratitude technique.

My invitation to you today is…

Simply become aware of the stories you are telling yourself about your body. That's it. Don't try to change them. Don't tell yourself they're wrong. Don't beat yourself up about it. Treat it as a chance to practise awareness and acceptance. What are your body-stories?

Affirmation:

I am grateful for everything my body does for me, even if it wobbles or creaks!

Affirmation: "I am grateful for everything my body does for me, no matter even if it wobbles or creaks!"

Week 35: Day 1 ~ *Today I am grateful for...*   *Date:*

In your week 35 podcast I share with you a secret about how your body knows the answer to every decision you will ever need to make – and how you can connect with its wisdom. It's surprisingly easy.

Week 35: Day 2 ~ *Today I am grateful for...*   *Date:*

Week 35: Day 3 ~ *Today I am grateful for…*   *Date:*

Week 35: Day 4 ~ *Today I am grateful for…*   *Date:*

Affirmation: "I am grateful for everything my body does for me, no matter even if it wobbles or creaks!"

Week 35: Day 5 ~ *Today I am grateful for…*   *Date:*

Week 35: Day 6 ~ *Today I am grateful for…*   *Date:*

Week 35: Day 7 ~ *Today I am grateful for…*   *Date:*

Pause for a moment to take a snapshot (see page 12). You can use this space to make any notes. I'd love to hear how you're getting on, over at the readers' club forum.

"Reflect upon your present blessings, of which every man has plenty; not on your past misfortunes of which all men have some." - *Charles Dickens*

Week 36: Day 1 ~ *Today I am grateful for…*   *Date:*

In the week 36 podcast episode you're going to get to write a very special thank you letter.

Week 36: Day 2 ~ *Today I am grateful for…*   *Date:*

Don't make your happiness dependent on future gifts; life is too short to waste another moment without appreciating what you already have.

Week 36: Day 3 ~ *Today I am grateful for…*   *Date:*

Week 36: Day 4 ~ *Today I am grateful for…*   *Date:*

Affirmation: "I am grateful for everything my body does for me, no matter even if it wobbles or creaks!"

Week 36: Day 5 ~ *Today I am grateful for...*   *Date:*

Week 36: Day 6 ~ *Today I am grateful for...*   *Date:*

Affirmation: "I am grateful for everything my body does for me, even if it wobbles or creaks!"

Week 36: Day 7 ~ *Today I am grateful for…*   *Date:*

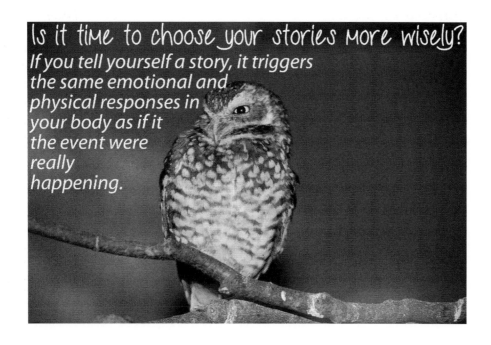

Is it time to choose your stories more wisely?
If you tell yourself a story, it triggers the same emotional and physical responses in your body as if it the event were really happening.

Being Grateful For Your Body

 How did you get on with spotting your body-stories? Any that you liked? Any that you'd like to shift? How about picking one specific story that you'd like to work with for the next gratitude project? We're talking about this over in the readers' club forum.

Today we're moving on to a technique that can really help to make a difference.

But, before we start, I want to reassure you that whatever your current body-stories are, that's ok. This isn't about 'getting rid' of them, or changing them. It's about choosing new stories – some that are more empowering, more uplifting, more motivating, based on gratitude and love, rather than fear and rejection.

Changing Your Body Stories – With Gratitude:

1. During the day today, pause at a random point to notice what you body is doing for you in that moment.

2. Become aware of the part of your body that is the 'leader' in that moment and say 'thank you' to it.

3. Allow that feeling of gratitude to gently fill that area of your body – and to flow throughout your Being. Allow yourself to smile and relax.

4. It doesn't matter whether your body was brushing your teeth or taking you up the stairs at work, or reading this message say 'thank you' to it.

5. Repeat this at random points during your day and you'll soon be retraining your Monkey Mind to focus on feeling grateful for your body.

Affirmation:

To each and every function in my body, I say 'Thank you!'

Week 37: Day 1 ~ *Today I am grateful for…*   *Date:*

 In your week 37 podcast you'll unlock the power to listen to what your body *really* wants and you'll discover why not being able to do this is what can keep us stuck in unhealthy habits.

Week 37: Day 2 ~ *Today I am grateful for…*   *Date:*

When you shift to sending gratitude to your body, you shift the chemical and hormone balance in your cells back towards healing.

Week 37: Day 3 ~ *Today I am grateful for…*   *Date:*

Week 37: Day 4 ~ *Today I am grateful for…*   *Date:*

Your body does so much more for you than anything else on this planet. Could you take a minute out to say 'thank you' to it today?

Week 37: Day 5 ~ *Today I am grateful for…*   *Date:*

Week 37: Day 6 ~ *Today I am grateful for…*   *Date:*

Affirmation: "To each and every function in my body, I say 'Thank you'!"

Week 37: Day 7 ~ *Today I am grateful for…*   *Date:*

Week 38: Day 1 ~ *Today I am grateful for…*   *Date:*

 The week 38 podcast brings you a fantastic practical technique that can transform your relationship with your body – with gratitude.

Week 38: Day 2 ~ *Today I am grateful for…*   *Date:*

Week 38: Day 3 ~ *Today I am grateful for…*   *Date:*

Practising gratitude, little and often, helps us to tread the path to reconnect with our inner peace and love, one step at a time.

Affirmation: "To each and every function in my body, I say 'Thank you'!"

Week 38: Day 4 ~ *Today I am grateful for…*   *Date:*

Week 38: Day 5 ~ *Today I am grateful for…*   *Date:*

Week 38: Day 6 ~ *Today I am grateful for…*   *Date:*

Week 38: Day 7 ~ *Today I am grateful for…*   *Date:*

You can breathe in; you can breathe out. That miracle of life is worthy of your gratitude. Everything else is a bonus.

Breathing With Gratitude

Sometimes gratitude can feel tough, especially if your mind is racing. So today I'd like to share with you a really simple, yet potentially profound, mindful breathing technique that can create beautiful shifts in your body, mind and emotions.

It's a meditation that can be done in one minute or ten –wonderfully de-stressing!

1. Start by sitting with your back fairly straight. Imagine a thread pulling through the crown of your head, gently lengthening your spine, allowing a space to form between each vertebra. You're not looking for ramrod straight; you're looking for gentle, natural curves, with a relaxed stretch. And as that thread draws up through the crown of your head, gently lengthening the lumbar spine, all the way up to the thoracic spine, and the neck… tucking the chin under slightly, to elongate the back of the neck and release any tension.

    … … …

2. Breathe in deeply, through your nose, and breathe out through your mouth with an 'ahhh' sighing sound, releasing tension and stress. Do this 3 times. Feel the tension melting away… Softly close your eyes and allow a gentle half-smile to rest on your face.

3. For the next few moments, I'd like you just to let your awareness – focus – your attention – rest on your breathing; accepting your breathing and not trying to change it in any way.

    … … …

4. And if your mind wanders, how about giving it a job? Bringing your awareness back to your breath… and this time, as you breathe in, consciously choosing to think: *Thank you for my life-giving breath*; and as you breathe out: *Thank you for my life-giving breath*…

    … … …

5. I invite you to really connect with the organs and the muscles and other parts of your body that allow you to breathe; and as you breathe in and out, saying a silent 'thank you' to your diaphragm… to your lungs… all of the muscles and the tendons… and everything else that allows you to breathe… whether breathing is effortless for you… or whether sometimes it's more of a challenge… Thank you diaphragm… Thank you lungs… Thank you body… Thank you breath…

    … … …

6. And allow that sense of gratitude to grow… as your breath fills your body with life-giving energy… and the out-breath carries away the old by-products and toxins… allow that thank you to flow through every oxygenated cell in your body…

7. When you're ready... it's time to release today's practice... making sure your feet are flat on the ground, imagine you're growing roots from the soles of your feet, deep into the earth... and these roots are connecting you with the earth beneath you... breathing in from the earth... breathing out into the earth... and you might see those roots; you might feel them physically; you might even hear them as they grow... and when you have a strong sense of those roots, anchoring you into the earth, take a deep sighing breath... a little stretch.

8. Keeping your eyes gently closed... rubbing the palms of your hands together, creating some warmth... and when you can feel that warmth, cupping that warmth over your gently closed eyes... opening your eyes behind those hands and gently spreading your fingers, to let the light in, bit by bit... rubbing your face... a good stretch and a good yawn! Thank you... That's your "Thank you breath" meditation. I wish you a wonderful day!

Affirmation:

Thank you for my breath.

Week 39: Day 1 ~ *Today I am grateful for...*   *Date:*

 Your week 39 podcast guides you through the little-known benefits of simple belly-breathing and how you can use this to cut your stress levels, any time, any place.

Affirmation: "Thank you for my breath."

Week 39: Day 2 ~ *Today I am grateful for...*   *Date:*

Week 39: Day 3 ~ *Today I am grateful for...*   *Date:*

If you let the sound of your breath be 'thank you', then your thoughts, words and deeds will always flow from your heart.

Week 39: Day 4 ~ *Today I am grateful for…*   *Date:*

Week 39: Day 5 ~ *Today I am grateful for…*   *Date:*

Affirmation: "Thank you for my breath."

Week 39: Day 6 ~ *Today I am grateful for…*   *Date:*

Week 39: Day 7 ~ *Today I am grateful for…*   *Date:*

Week 40: Day 1 ~ *Today I am grateful for…*   *Date:*

 The week 40 podcast brings you one of my favourite *pranayama* (special yogic breathing) techniques that can help you feel more clearly, even if you're feeling stressed and overwhelmed.

Week 40: Day 2 ~ *Today I am grateful for…*   *Date:*

Practising gratitude makes it easier to smile, even if
it feels as though the rain will never cease.

Week 40: Day 3 ~ *Today I am grateful for…*   *Date:*

Week 40: Day 4 ~ *Today I am grateful for…*   *Date:*

The grumbles and complaints that run through your mind mask your true inner radiance. Heart-felt gratitude is a way of uncovering it again, so you can create a pathway back home.

Week 40: Day 5 ~ *Today I am grateful for…*   *Date:*

Week 40: Day 6 ~ *Today I am grateful for…*   *Date:*

Week 40: Day 7 ~ *Today I am grateful for…*   *Date:*

 Pause for a moment to take a snapshot (see page 12). You can use this space to make any notes. I'd love to hear how you're getting on, over at the readers' club forum!

How To Turn Your Words Around

There's a gratitude technique you can use to help you in any situation where you're finding it hard to figure out how to put your point across – especially if your relationship with the other person is less than perfect. But before we dive in, I'd like you to try something out for a moment:

- Imagine thinking of a food you really hate – something you would refuse, even if you were really hungry... Remind yourself of all the times your Mum / Grannie / School Dinner Lady tried to force you to eat it... Feel it... See it... Smell it... Yuck!

  Now imagine bumping into an old friend and telling them what you have been up to lately... What kinds of stories do you tell?

  Give yourself a shake to let go of that feeling!

- Now think of a food you really enjoy – one that you feel happy about eating, which brings back good memories... Remember some of the best times you had eating it... Feel how those memories bring a smile to your face... Let those feelings flow through your body... See that food... Smell it... Taste it...

  Now imagine bumping into an old friend and telling them what you have been up to lately... What kinds of stories do you tell?

How were the two scenarios different? Did you notice how much easier it is to tell happy stories and to speak clearly, when you were feeling full of happy thoughts?

The tone of your thoughts directly impact your words.

Of course, I'm not advocating that you go round spending your whole day thinking about food – it would be unlikely to have a positive impact on your waistline. But imagine how shifting your thoughts to come from a place of gratitude, rather than anger or fear, could change the words you share with others?

When we retrain our Monkey Mind to put more energy into stories of gratitude than into complaining, it shifts the way we interact with the world. We're less subjected to our stress hormones and less likely to be only able to access the primitive stress-response part of our brain, making it easier to think and speak clearly. Also, a background chatter of happier thoughts means we more readily share happy stories and comments with others, rather than moaning and criticising. So for our next gratitude technique, I invite you to do something very simple, but potentially life-changing:

> *The next time you catch yourself about to say something negative or angry or unkind, press the 'pause' button in your brain by taking a slow breath, and then think back to one of the things you have felt grateful for lately. Now, when you speak, you might find that what you want to say has changed!*

Affirmation:

I choose to let my thoughts of gratitude filter through into my words.

Affirmation: "I choose to let my thoughts of gratitude filter through into my words"

Week 41: Day 1 ~ *Today I am grateful for…*   *Date:*

Your week 41 podcast lets you in on the secret of the two most powerful words that most of us use every day, which have the power to crank up your confidence or leave you drowning in self-doubt. P.S. Let's turn that around!

Week 41: Day 2 ~ *Today I am grateful for…*   *Date:*

"Let us be grateful to people who make us happy; they are the charming gardeners who make our souls blossom." - Marcel Proust

Week 41: Day 3 ~ *Today I am grateful for…*   *Date:*

Week 41: Day 4 ~ *Today I am grateful for…*   *Date:*

Affirmation: "I choose to let my thoughts of gratitude filter through into my words"

Week 41: Day 5 ~ *Today I am grateful for…*   *Date:*

Week 41: Day 6 ~ *Today I am grateful for…*   *Date:*

Week 41: Day 7 ~ *Today I am grateful for…*   *Date:*

We often don't notice the improvements we have made and the changes that our gratitude practices have brought to our life until...

we re-read what we wrote in our journal several weeks or months before.

Is it time to review your journal?

Week 42: Day 1 ~ *Today I am grateful for…*   *Date:*

The week 42 podcast talks about why there's no point in beating yourself up and reminds you of a super-simple process you already know from A Year Full Of Gratitude to turn that around – fast.

Week 42: Day 2 ~ *Today I am grateful for…*   *Date:*

Week 42: Day 3 ~ *Today I am grateful for...*   *Date:*

Week 42: Day 4 ~ *Today I am grateful for...*   *Date:*

One of our deepest needs is to be appreciated. So how about giving that gift to someone today?

Affirmation: "I choose to let my thoughts of gratitude filter through into my words"

Week 42: Day 5 ~ *Today I am grateful for...*   *Date:*

Week 42: Day 6 ~ *Today I am grateful for...*   *Date:*

Gratitude turns every-day life into a series of blessings and miracles.

Affirmation: "I choose to let my thoughts of gratitude filter through into my words."

Week 42: Day 7 ~ *Today I am grateful for…*   *Date:*

How are you getting on?

Do you have any successes to celebrate? Any insights or lightbulbs to share? Could you support someone else? Remember you can get answers to your questions, share your insights and connect with others on a gratitude journey, plus get bonus videos, MP3s, articles and more, over at the Readers' Club – www.ClareJosa.com/GratitudeClub

How To Feel Grateful For Your Monkey Mind

Now there's an idea... How much effort do we put into fighting our Monkey Mind? And does it work? Or does it cunningly use even more clever tricks to get our attention?

Earlier in this journal, I shared a quote from Marcus Aurelius: "The happiness of your life depends on the quality of your thoughts."

I remember a dear friend, about a decade ago, asking me how on earth she could shift her thoughts from negative to positive, when she had spent a lifetime training herself to think about the bad bits.

Much of my work over the past ten years has been invested in finding simple, practical, highly effective answers to her question. It's one of the reasons I decided to create this gratitude journal.

The quality of our thoughts has a profound impact on our experience of life. But telling your Monkey Mind to stop thinking thoughts that make you feel miserable doesn't work. Why?

Because your mind can't process a 'negative'.

What do I mean? I mean that if you shout at a child, "Don't run!" it first has to imagine 'running' and then the 'not', by which time the fall has probably happened. If you tell them, "Don't fall over!" then they first have to imagine falling over, and you can guess the rest.

Tell your Monkey Mind, "Don't think negative thoughts!" and it first has to imagine the 'negative thoughts' bit and… you guessed it… it never gets round to processing the "don't"!

So instead of trying to 'get rid' of 'negative' thoughts, how about accepting them and sending them love and gratitude, before releasing them and moving on to the next thought? And if it's a happy one, thank it for hanging around. Then let it go. There's no need to cling to it.

You're not trying to 'banish' the sad or angry thoughts. You're simply looking to tip the balance in favour of the happy and more empowering ones, one day at a time; one thought at a time.

 And what better way to do it than to tune yourself in to gratitude? There's a bonus meditation waiting for you in the readers' club to help you experience feeling grateful for your monkey mind! You'll find it at the Week 43 tab.

Affirmation:

I choose to feel grateful for my Monkey Mind.

Week 43: Day 1 ~ *Today I am grateful for…*   *Date:*

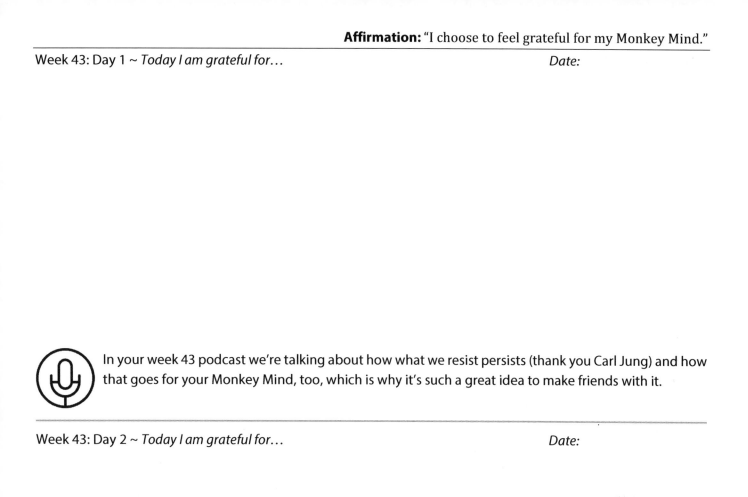

In your week 43 podcast we're talking about how what we resist persists (thank you Carl Jung) and how that goes for your Monkey Mind, too, which is why it's such a great idea to make friends with it.

Week 43: Day 2 ~ *Today I am grateful for…*   *Date:*

Affirmation: "I choose to feel grateful for my Monkey Mind."

Week 43: Day 3 ~ *Today I am grateful for…*   *Date:*

Week 43: Day 4 ~ *Today I am grateful for…*   *Date:*

The simple act of genuine, unconditional gratitude has the power to change your life.

Week 43: Day 5 ~ *Today I am grateful for…*   *Date:*

Week 43: Day 6 ~ *Today I am grateful for…*   *Date:*

"Gratitude is riches. Complaint is poverty." - Doris Day

Affirmation: "I choose to feel grateful for my Monkey Mind."

Week 43: Day 7 ~ *Today I am grateful for…*   *Date:*

Week 44: Day 1 ~ *Today I am grateful for…*   *Date:*

 In your week 44 podcast we're talking about 'unconditional gratitude' – gratitude without attachment or agenda, and why 'conditional gratitude' can be such a hard habit to break.

Week 44: Day 2 ~ *Today I am grateful for…*   *Date:*

Week 44 Day 3: ~ *Today I am grateful for…*   *Date:*

Affirmation: "I choose to feel grateful for my Monkey Mind."

Week 44: Day 4 ~ *Today I am grateful for…*   *Date:*

Week 44: Day 5 ~ *Today I am grateful for…*   *Date:*

Some days it feels easy, other days it's more of a challenge. But either way, gratitude sets the tone for your day and gives a clear instruction to your unconscious mind that its job is to find more things to feel good about.

202

Week 44: Day 6 ~ *Today I am grateful for…*   *Date:*

Week 44: Day 7 ~ *Today I am grateful for…*   *Date:*

Walking With Gratitude

Today I'd like to share with you one of my favourite mindfulness techniques, which can easily be transformed into a super-portable do-it-while-you're-busy gratitude technique: mindful walking. Walking mindfully is a massive topic, and can be done in many ways, so today I'm going to share with you the core of the technique, for you to experiment with adding a new flavour to your gratitude practices.

START: This walking can be done anywhere – outside in nature or even walking up the stairs or around your kitchen. Choose somewhere that you can be on your own, for the first few times.

1. Take a 'snapshot' of how you are feeling – physically, emotionally, mind-wise. We'll come back to this.

2. Start walking. Slow your speed down by at least 10%. This makes it easier to concentrate.

3. Focus all of your awareness on your feet. Become fully aware of the physical sensations of your feet on the floor, as they connect with the Earth.
   [Doing this barefoot on grass or sand is a special treat - though not essential!]

4. If your attention wanders, gently guide it back to the physical feeling of your feet on the earth.
   - When you're in the rhythm of it, choose to spend 30 seconds or a minute, becoming aware of the physical sensations in your body. Say a silent 'thank you' to your body.
   - Notice your balance – just feel those amazing muscles, tendons, ligaments, bones, joints and nerves doing such an incredible job of keeping you safe and upright. Say a silent 'thank you' to your body.
   - Notice your arms moving – you don't have to change anything; just become fully aware of the physical movement. Say a silent 'thank you' to your body.
   - Notice your posture. Feel the physical sensations, if you tweak the way you are holding your body. Say a silent 'thank you' to your body.
   - Really feel the soles of your feet with each step, as they take your weight as you walk. Say a silent 'thank you' to your body.
   - Then, when you're ready, return to simply being aware of each step, connecting with the Earth. Say a silent 'thank you' to the Earth.

END: when you feel ready, release your practice and take that snapshot again. How are you feeling – physically, emotionally, mind-wise? Compare that to the snapshot from the beginning. With practice, you'll notice that mindful walking makes a tangible difference.

Affirmation:

I feel grateful for the Earth beneath my feet.

Week 45: Day 1 ~ *Today I am grateful for…*   *Date:*

In your week 45 podcast you'll discover why gratitude and mindfulness (our last two techniques) make such good companions – and how you can use this to create techniques of your own.

Week 45: Day 2 ~ *Today I am grateful for…*   *Date:*

Affirmation: "I feel grateful for the Earth beneath my feet."

Week 45: Day 3 ~ *Today I am grateful for...*   *Date:*

Week 45: Day 4 ~ *Today I am grateful for...*   *Date:*

Week 45: Day 5 ~ *Today I am grateful for…*   *Date:*

Week 45: Day 6 ~ *Today I am grateful for…*   *Date:*

"Walk as though your feet are kissing the earth." – Thich Nhat Hanh

Week 45: Day 6 ~ *Today I am grateful for…*   *Date:*

 Pause for a moment to take a snapshot (see page 12). You can use this space to make any notes. I'd love to hear from you over at the readers' club forum!

Week 45: Day 7 ~ *Today I am grateful for…*   *Date:*

Week 46: Day 1 ~ *Today I am grateful for…*   *Date:*

 Your week 46 podcast gives you the opportunity to experience how truly supported you are – it's something we all-too-often struggle with.

Affirmation: "I feel grateful for the Earth beneath my feet."

Week 46: Day 2 ~ *Today I am grateful for…*   *Date:*

Week 46: Day 3 ~ *Today I am grateful for…*   *Date:*

Week 46: Day 4 ~ *Today I am grateful for…*   *Date:*

Week 46: Day 5 ~ *Today I am grateful for…*   *Date:*

"Blessed are those that can give without remembering and receive without forgetting." - Anonymous

Affirmation: "I feel grateful for the Earth beneath my feet."

Week 46: Day 6 ~ *Today I am grateful for…*   *Date:*

Week 46: Day 7 ~ *Today I am grateful for…*   *Date:*

Treating Your Body Like The Temple Of Your Soul

Today, I want to ask you a question:

How different would each moment of your day feel, if you treated your body as though you were grateful for it; if you truly considered it to be the Temple Of Your Soul?

Allow that question to wash through you for a few moments...

- How would you sit?
- How would you stand?
- How would you move?
- What kinds of thoughts would you be thinking?
- What would you eat and drink?
- How would you breathe?

Allow yourself to pause for a few moments and really consider your answer to these questions. Let the answers bubble up. Really dive into the experience.

And, guess what?

Now you have imagined it, you can be it.

It's as simple as choosing to flick a switch. You just imagined – and created – your very own action plan for shifting how you experience your body. Cool, eh? Give gratitude to your body, treating it like the temple of your soul, and it will reward you every day, for the rest of your life.

If I believed that my body is the temple of my soul, would I eat this?
Would I do that?

Can you imagine how that might influence your choices? Notice how much easier it is to feel grateful to your body, if you consider it to be the temple of your soul? We're talking about this in the readers' club forum.

 There's a bonus video waiting for you under the 'Week 47' tab in the readers' club: "Aches & Pains – The Gratitude Solution". I'd love to hear how you get on with it, over in the forum.

Affirmation:

I feel grateful for my body and treat it as the temple of my soul.

Week 47: Day 1 ~ *Today I am grateful for…*   *Date:*

In your week 47 podcast I share with you my favourite technique for getting out of my head and back into my body – it's a near-instant stress-ditcher and it can help bring your gratitude practice to life.

Week 47: Day 2 ~ *Today I am grateful for…*   *Date:*

Week 47: Day 3 ~ *Today I am grateful for…*   *Date:*

Week 47: Day 4 ~ *Today I am grateful for…*   *Date:*

Don't dismiss aches and pains. Thank them. They're your body's way of letting
you know that something needs to change.

Affirmation: "I feel grateful for my body and treat it as the temple of my soul."

Week 47: Day 5 ~ *Today I am grateful for…*   *Date:*

Week 47: Day 6 ~ *Today I am grateful for…*   *Date:*

Affirmation: "I feel grateful for my body and treat it as the temple of my soul.."

Week 47: Day 7 ~ *Today I am grateful for…*   *Date:*

Week 48: Day 1 ~ *Today I am grateful for…*   *Date:*

 Your week 48 podcast shares a strategy to bring gratitude for your body into each and every mundane activity during your day. It's surprisingly life-changing.

Week 48: Day 2 ~ *Today I am grateful for…*   *Date:*

Week 48: Day 3 ~ *Today I am grateful for…*   *Date:*

How about using the act of getting dressed as a chance to say 'thank you' to each part of your body, in turn? How might that shift your day?

Week 48: Day 4 ~ *Today I am grateful for…*   *Date:*

Week 48: Day 5 ~ *Today I am grateful for…*   *Date:*

Say 'thank you' for the little things and they may soon become the big things.

Affirmation: "I feel grateful for my body and treat it as the temple of my soul."

Week 48: Day 6 ~ *Today I am grateful for…*   *Date:*

Week 48: Day 7 ~ *Today I am grateful for…*   *Date:*

Gratitude For All You Have To Give

As we move towards the end of this year of your gratitude journal (Where did the time go?), we are moving on to a topic that many of us try to avoid. Here's some inspiration from Marianne Williamson, to kick us off:

Our deepest fear is not that we are inadequate. Our deepest fear is that we are powerful beyond measure.

It is our light, not our darkness that most frightens us.

We ask ourselves, 'Who am I to be brilliant, gorgeous, talented, fabulous?' Actually, who are you not to be?

"Why am I here? What is the purpose of my life?" We spend decades looking for the answers to those questions. Yet the answers were there, waiting for you, deep down inside, all along. Why are you here?

To be the boldest, strongest, most vibrant expression of **you** *that you can be.*

You are what your world needs. The things you love doing, the things that make your heart sing, the things that would make you jump out of bed on a grey and rainy day, are woven into the purpose of your life.

Your life's purpose doesn't require you to give up your job, live in a cave and meditate all day (ok, most likely not!). It requires you to tune in to your unique gifts, to consciously choose to cultivate what you feel passionate about and to let go of the fears that have prevented you from being who you really are, wherever you are and whoever you are with.

How can gratitude help you with all of this?

By saying 'thank you' for your gifts and talents, instead of running from them!

1. Take three deep breaths, with a sigh as you breathe out, to release tension and come back to this moment.

2. Tune in to your heart and ask yourself: "What do I love doing?" Let the answers bubble up, without judgement or analysis.

3. As each answer bubbles up, say a heart-felt 'thank you' to yourself, for whatever it is you love.

4. Make a commitment to yourself to create the time and space to enjoy something from that list, every day, even if just for sixty seconds. It will transform your life.

Affirmation: (with a wink to Marianne, again!)
I choose to let my light shine, giving others permission to do the same.

Affirmation: "I choose to let my light shine, giving others permission to do the same."

Week 49: Day 1 ~ *Today I am grateful for…*   *Date:*

Your week 49 podcast is all about your superpowers – your inner genius. Learn how to uncover them and discover why we're usually so scared to 'own' them!

Week 49: Day 2 ~ *Today I am grateful for…*   *Date:*

"The best things in life aren't things." – Art Buchwald

Week 49: Day 3 ~ *Today I am grateful for…*   *Date:*

Week 49: Day 4 ~ *Today I am grateful for…*   *Date:*

Affirmation: "I choose to let my light shine, giving others permission to do the same."

Week 49: Day 5 ~ *Today I am grateful for…*   *Date:*

Week 49: Day 6 ~ *Today I am grateful for…*   *Date:*

Affirmation: "I choose to let my light shine, giving others permission to do the same."

Week 49: Day 7 ~ *Today I am grateful for…*   *Date:*

Whatever happens in life, we can choose to tell ourselves stories about the thorns; or we can choose to tell ourselves stories about the roses. Which are you choosing today?

Week 50: Day 1 ~ *Today I am grateful for…*   *Date:*

Here in week 50 we're connecting with your Big Vision – the difference you're here to make in the world – with gratitude.

Week 50: Day 2 ~ *Today I am grateful for…*   *Date:*

There is more to life than increasing its speed." - *Gandhi*

Week 50: Day 3 ~ *Today I am grateful for…*   *Date:*

Week 50: Day 4 ~ *Today I am grateful for…*   *Date:*

Affirmation: "I choose to let my light shine, giving others permission to do the same."

Week 50: Day 5 ~ *Today I am grateful for...*   *Date:*

Week 50: Day 6 ~ *Today I am grateful for...*   *Date:*

Someone out there is waiting for you – for the unique gifts you bring to serve the world. The world is waiting for you to let your inner diamond shine.

Affirmation: "I choose to let my light shine, giving others permission to do the same."

Week 50: Day 7 ~ *Today I am grateful for…*   *Date:*

Pause for a moment to take a snapshot (see page 12). You can use this space to make any notes. I'd love to hear how you're getting on, over at the readers' club forum.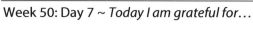

And Finally... Gratitude To Yourself, For Taking This Journey

I'm wondering about the massive variety of things, people and experiences that you have given gratitude for, over the past year.

I'm guessing that, if we were to look at everyone who has been joining in with this journal, we would be amazed at how many things there are to feel grateful for.

But I'm curious: how often did you give gratitude for yourself?

I know we did gratitude for our bodies and our breathing and our thoughts, but how often did you – the 'you deep down inside' – make it onto the pages of your journal?

For each and every time you wrote in your journal – thank you.

For every time you practised one of the techniques – thank you.

For each and every time you share your experiences, whether in the Readers' Club or with friends and family – thank you.

For the changes and shifts you have made – thank you.

For the dedication you shown in getting to this stage – thank you.

For everything you have done, to help create a powerful wave of gratitude that can spread around the world – thank you.

My invitation to you for the final few weeks of this journal is a simple, yet potentially profound, one:

Choose to do and think things, every day, that your 'future self' will thank you for.

The 'you' sitting here now has a lot for which to thank the 'you' 11 ½ months ago, who made the choice to start this journal. When you look at all you have experienced and how your life has shifted over the past months, today's 'you' wouldn't be who you now are, without the efforts of the previous 'yous'.

If you make the conscious choice, each day, to do and say and experience things for which the future you will feel grateful, just imagine how life will be! And, as I've said before: if you can imagine it, you can create it! See you 'there'!

Affirmation:
I choose to do and think things, every day, that my future self will thank me for.

Week 51: Day 1 ~ *Today I am grateful for…* Date:

Your week 51 podcast is all about owning your 'amazingness' and letting your light shine.

Week 51: Day 2 ~ *Today I am grateful for…* Date:

Week 51: Day 3 ~ *Today I am grateful for…*   *Date:*

Week 51: Day 4 ~ *Today I am grateful for…*   *Date:*

Week 51: Day 5 ~ *Today I am grateful for…*   *Date:*

Week 51: Day 6 ~ *Today I am grateful for…*   *Date:*

At times our own light goes out and is rekindled by a spark from another person. Each of us has cause to think with deep gratitude of those who have lighted the flame within us.. - Albert Schweitzer

Week 51: Day 7 ~ *Today I am grateful for...*   *Date:*

Week 52: Day 1 ~ *Today I am grateful for...*   *Date:*

 In this penultimate episode of the Year Full Of Gratitude podcast, I share with you my personal strategy for using gratitude to create the future I have been dreaming of.

Week 52: Day 2 ~ *Today I am grateful for…*   *Date:*

Week 52: Day 3 ~ *Today I am grateful for…*   *Date:*

Affirmation: "I choose to do and think things, every day, that my future self will thank me for."

Week 52: Day 4 ~ *Today I am grateful for…*   *Date:*

Week 52: Day 5 ~ *Today I am grateful for…*   *Date:*

Gratitude is like flicking a switch, helping you to see what is there, rather than what is missing.

Week 52: Day 6 ~ *Today I am grateful for…*   *Date:*

Week 52: Day 7 ~ *Today I am grateful for…*   *Date:*

We've got one more week together! Yes, you're getting a bonus Week 53. But before we dive in, it's time for another snapshot (page 12). What has changed for you? Let me know via the readers' club forum!

Week 53: Day 1 ~ *Today I am grateful for...*   *Date:*

 In our final podcast episode – week 53 – you'll get ninja tips for keeping your gratitude habit going, for taking things to the next level with your self-talk and for consciously creating the life you have been dreaming of.

Week 53: Day 2 ~ *Today I am grateful for...*   *Date:*

Week 53: Day 3 ~ *Today I am grateful for...*   *Date:*

"Do not spoil what you have by desiring what you have not; remember that what you now have was once among the things you only hoped for." - Epicurus

Week 53: Day 4 ~ *Today I am grateful for…*   *Date:*

Week 53: Day 5 ~ *Today I am grateful for…*   *Date:*

"We must find time to stop and thank the people who make a difference in our lives." - John F. Kennedy

Week 53: Day 6 ~ *Today I am grateful for…*   *Date:*

Week 53: Day 7 ~ *Today I am grateful for…*   *Date:*

Wrapping Up – How Have Things Shifted For You This Year?

 Congratulations! It's a year on from when you started your gratitude journal. It's time to review how things have shifted for you? How about repeating the exercise from page 9 and noticing how your answers have move on? I'd love to hear from you in the readers' club forum.

1. Which emotions do you feel most often, during a typical day?

2. How would you describe your stress levels?

3. What kinds of thoughts does your mind typically think?

4. How would you describe your energy levels and your physical health?

5. Why are you choosing to practise gratitude?

6. If you could make one change in your life, what would it be?

7. How will you know when you have made that change?

8. If you could give one piece of advice to yourself, right here, right now, what would it be?

9. Knowing what you now know, and having experienced the how gratitude has shifted your experience of life over the past year, how do you want to shift your life, over the coming 12 months? What is your vision for the 'future you'? What steps will you take, each day, to move you there? How will life feel, when you get there?

Being cheeky:

Why bother waiting for that feeling? How about diving into it, right now, and making those shifts in this moment?

How To Keep Your Gratitude Habit Going

Do you want to take your experience of gratitude to the next level?

10. How are you going to make sure you continue to weave gratitude into your daily life?

11. How will you keep yourself motivated?

12. How could you spread the word about gratitude to a wider audience, sharing the gifts you have experienced?

Today's choices create your tomorrows.

With each and every thought, you can choose again.

With each and every breath, you can choose thoughts that inspire you and make your heart sing.

Wishing you love and laughter.

Namaste.

About Clare Josa

I'm guessing we 'know' each other pretty well by now, but just in case you want some background blurb, here it is!

I have been mentoring Passionate World-Changers since 2002. As an entrepreneur myself, the creator of over fifteen years' of online and face-to-face training courses, and the author of 5 non-fiction books and two novels, I know about the hidden blocks that keep us stuck, dreaming big, but playing small. I have been through most of them, myself.

But as an NLP Trainer and long-time breakthrough mentor, I also know how to get past them, and have helped many thousands of people, just like you, to do exactly that. I specialise in being able to spot the smallest changes that will produce the biggest results for you, and in sharing solutions with you in a way that makes it super-easy for you to learn and apply them, no matter how busy you are - or how much your monkey mind might object.

I used to be an engineer (I have a Master's Degree in Mechanical Engineering And German), but I'm also a certified Meditation & Yoga teacher, so I love demystifying Ancient Wisdom into practical actions you can take in less time than it takes to boil a kettle. My clients call it 'engineer-approved woo-woo'. And it all comes with a bucket load of common sense and a generous dollop of humour. My clients call it 'engineer-approved woo-woo'.

I know about being busy, too. I'm a mum of 3 young boys, I run my own business and have a passion for dancing like a crazy thing to loud music in my kitchen. If I can find the time to write this book, you can find the time to go through the techniques in it - and I'll even help you with that shortly, because I know what a block it can be.

If I had a superpower (more on that in step 1), my clients would say it's bringing intuitive clarity to where confusion and chaos previously reigned, combining with inspiration and enthusiasm.

Want to keep working together? I'd love to hear from you. You can choose from reading my other books, taking an online course, joining me for a workshop, joining a mastermind or working one-to-one. I also speak at events about how to change the world by changing yourself:

www.ClareJosa.com/work-with-clare-josa/

Before I sign off, I'd like to say a huge thank you to you for sharing your journey with me. No matter how often you have practised these techniques, you will have taken you a step closer towards the life you want. None of it is wasted. It all makes a difference. Thank you!

Wishing you inner peace and happiness on your journey.

With love, Namaste,

Clare

www.ClareJosa.com

More Books By Clare Josa

You can order Clare's books from the big bookshop in the sky or from your local bookstore.

Non-Fiction:

Dare To Dream Bigger

ISBN 978-1-908854-79-7

On a mission to change the world?

Dare to Dream Bigger brings you step-by-step how-to with its unique blend of proven business strategy and little-known 'inside work'.

It's time to ditch those secret 3am fears, so you can make the difference you are **really** here to make in the world - and fall in love with the journey.

52 Mindful Moments

ISBN 978-1908854-44-5

Want to feel less stressed, happier, calmer and more at peace, but you don't have the time?

What if all it took to change your life was one mindful minute? Could you spare that long?

The inspirational mindfulness techniques in 52 Mindful Moments will help you to shift away from feeling stressed, worried and exhausted, to feeling calmer, happier, more at peace and more alive, in under sixty seconds.

Fiction

You Take Yourself With You

Book 1 of The Denucci Deception

ISBN 978-1-908-85488-9

Sophie is hungry for promotion, but when she rejects her new boss's advances, he sets out to destroy more than her career. As her life falls apart, she tries to escape the black cloud that threatens to overwhelm her – with disastrous results. Will she wake up in time to find the happiness, success and love she secretly craves?

When Christof survives a car crash that kills his father, he inherits more than guilt. A mountain of hidden debt risks destroying the cherry farm his family has called home for generations. But Christof's work in Milan wants him to dig up dirt on the mafia – and distractions could be deadly. Can he save the farm, beat the mafia and learn one of life's most important lessons, before it's too late?

You Take Yourself With You is a journey of courage, hope, humour, love and realising that we're not alone.

First, Tell No Lies

Book 2 of The Denucci Deception

ISBN 978-1-908854-91-9

A chance encounter in an Italian backstreet will change two lives forever.

Set to testify against the mafia, Christof is torn between what he wants and doing the right thing. When his work asks him to double-cross a Camorra boss, he risks more than his own safety.

Sabotaging the very happiness she craves, Sophie juggles the relationship she has been dreaming of and a promotion that fills her with self-doubt, until a Tainted Diamond makes her number one on the camorra's hitlist. But she has no idea.

Will Christof finally admit the truth in time to save her life?

Acknowledgements

No gratitude journal would be complete without a few thank yous. I know you're keen to get on, so I'll keep it brief.

As ever, thank you to Peter and our boys for understanding all the times when I got up in the middle of the night or skipped meals, to pummel my laptop's keyboard or scribble colourful mind-maps, to create this book.

Thank you to my friends, across the globe, who helped to fire my enthusiasm for this project – and this fifth anniversary edition – and who helped me to have the dedication to finish it! Thank you to all who helped with proof-reading, trying out the exercises, giving feedback on the techniques and generally helping to fine-tune what you now see in front of you. And immense gratitude to the thousands of readers so far who have used the techniques in this book to change their lives and make a bigger difference in the world.

Thank you from the bottom of my heart to everyone who fell in love with the first edition of this book (Gratitude: A Daily Journal). The fact that you all dived in and played with the techniques – and asked questions and gave feedback – and used it all to change your life - is just so wonderful!

And, above all, thank you to **YOU** for making the promise to your future and working through A Year Full Of Gratitude and, in advance, for everything you do to help create a powerful wave of gratitude that can spread around the world.

With love, Namaste,

Clare. ♡

P.S. Please make sure you join the free Readers' Club so we can connect and share this journey. xx C.

www.ClareJosa.com/GratitudeClub

Icon credits: icons made by Smashicons, Freepik, Vitaly Gorbachev and Turkkub from flaticon.com. Thank you!

Index Of Gratitude Techniques

Index Of Affirmations

46391450R00141

Printed in Poland
by Amazon Fulfillment
Poland Sp. z o.o., Wrocław